## Praise for *There's a Moose in My Garden*

"A designer of exquisite gardens rarely shares her secrets for success, but in this book Brenda Adams shares those secrets, from initial idea to finishing touches. Now Alaska gardeners can be inspired by the first book dedicated to landscape design in the 49th state."
—*Julie Riley, horticulturist, University of Alaska Fairbanks Cooperative Extension Service*

"It's been nearly two decades since a book was written specifically for those of us who live and garden in Alaska. In *There's a Moose in My Garden*, Brenda Adams shows readers exactly how to create and enjoy lush ornamental gardens, and she sets readers off on solid footing with her plant list. She even highlights the use of foliage, bark, berries, and other details not every garden writer adequately promotes. *There's a Moose in My Garden* is a delightful and useful read for every Alaska gardener."
—*Annie Nevaldine, botanical photographer and master gardener*

"Anyone gardening in cold climates will miss a new classic by not reading *There's a Moose in My Garden*. Brenda Adams really does garden in Homer, Alaska, and she really does practice what she preaches. But I think it speaks to all gardeners in difficult places who soldier on with dedication and humor. I enjoyed it immensely."
—*Stephanie Cohen, award-winning writer and lecturer, a.k.a. "The Perennial Diva"*

"Experienced and novice gardeners alike will find *There's a Moose in My Garden* a must-read, while curious visitors are sure to find the book irresistible as well. This information-packed volume takes readers from plan to reality. The author stays with you through the entire process, like a mentor offering gentle advice. Irresistible."
—*C. Colston Burrell, garden designer, award-winning author, photographer, naturalist, and educator*

# There's a Moose in My Garden

# There's a Moose in My Garden

## Designing Gardens in Alaska and the Far North

Brenda C. Adams

University of Alaska Press
Fairbanks, Alaska

University of Alaska Press
P.O. Box 756240
Fairbanks, AK 99775-6240


Library of Congress Cataloging-in-Publication Data

Adams, Brenda C.
 There's a moose in my garden : designing gardens in Alaska and the Far North / by Brenda C. Adams.
    p. cm.
 Includes bibliographical references and index.
 ISBN 978-1-60223-208-2 (pbk. : alk. paper)
 1.  Gardening—Alaska. 2.  Gardens—Alaska—Design.  I. Title. II. Title: Designing gardens in Alaska and the
Far North.
 SB453.2.A4A33 2013
 635.09798—dc23
                                    2012048325


Cover and text design by Paula Elmes, ImageCraft Publications & Design.
Except where noted, all photos are the author's.

This publication was printed on acid-free paper that meets the minimum requirements for ANSI / NISO Z39.48–
1992 (R2002) (Permanence of Paper for Printed Library Materials).

Printed in the United States of America

# Contents

As a recovering Zone 4 gardener, I am both drawn to and repelled by gardens above forty-five degrees north latitude. Having retreated from Minnesota to Virginia and the warm climes of my youth, I revel in graceful springs, sustained autumns, and the precocious flowers of winter. I seldom think about the northern garden I left behind nearly sixteen years ago. Yet, reading *There's a Moose in My Garden* by Alaska gardener Brenda Adams arouses undeniable nostalgia. Vivid prose and opulent photos awaken memories of northern summer days when my garden was perfection.

As an outsider, I can't speak directly to the Alaska experience. Yet inherent in all northern gardeners is a sense of the inevitable. Up north, climate trumps all; you can't pretend that winter is a temporary inconvenience. The gift of sixty-degree winter days that I often experience in Virginia never happens in the north. Even a January thaw fails to reveal open ground, much less a few precious blooms.

So, deep in the ivory folds of winter's blanket, northern gardeners wait, read, plan, dream, and long for the return of flowers. Cue Brenda's book. *There's a Moose in My Garden* is an encouraging and humorous look at the challenges and joys of gardening in Alaska and the Far North. Sharing the accumulated wisdom of eighteen years in her garden on the Kenai Peninsula, Brenda delivers a practical yet inspirational guide with a deep reverence for her adopted homeland and enough levity to get through six months of cold winter darkness.

In no-nonsense prose, she makes it sound so effortless. Sure, there are challenges in the north. Early frost, late frost, winter temps well below zero, and summer temps that barely climb into the 70s. Then there are the voles, rabbits, and, of course, the moose. Brenda points out myriad joys as well. She can grow plants that are the envy of the vast majority of American gardeners: beguiling blue poppies, perfect primulas, and daunting delphiniums. Grrrrrr. Brenda takes the good, the bad, and the ugly all in stride and serves up a pragmatic guide filled with solid advice and practical techniques. In her own words, the "major purpose of this book is to help you create beautiful, healthy, and well-designed gardens in Alaska and the Far North."

This information-packed volume takes readers from plan to reality. The author stays with you through the entire process, like a mentor peering over your shoulder offering gentle guidance. Brenda explains how to envision and record your ideas in a logical progression using a base map. She takes you from spatial layout all the way through plant choices and artful combinations to create a finished garden plan. Along the way, she dispenses tips for blending your garden into the native landscape, often garden-like in its own right as wildflowers rush to meet the brief season of glory. Additional site-specific tips such as which annuals thrive without heat to initiate bloom, proper soil preparation, and many more make this book invaluable.

Combining plants requires years of experience to understand in any climate. Alaska, however, is unique among gardening climes due to the abbreviated growing season and the eternal daylight of summer. Brenda's illuminating assessments of perennials, grasses, shrubs, and vines are gleaned from personal experience in her own garden as well as dozens of gardens she designs and maintains for her clients. Gardening friends throughout Alaska also offered valuable input. The detailed species accounts help readers avoid the pitfalls of incorrect plant choice, as northern conditions render many traditional garden mainstays ineffective.

Few of us have ever had a real moose in the garden, but figuratively, we all have our moose stories. Bear, deer, elk, rabbit, skunk, whatever. No matter where we garden, we face challenges, and our indomitable spirit overcomes them. Experienced and novice residents alike will find *There's a Moose in My Garden* a must-read, while visitors curious about the vagaries of northern gardening are sure to find the book irresistible as well.

When the snow begins to fly and the coffee is piping hot, curl up with *There's a Moose in My Garden* and dream while you learn of the joys of gardening, Alaska style. Come mud season, you'll be well equipped to enter the garden, plan and trowel in hand, ready to begin.

C. Colston Burrell, Free Union, Virginia
December 2012

Gardening in Alaska, as well as most areas of the far northern latitudes, presents a multitude of special challenges, but more important, it offers unique opportunities and unexpected pleasures. There is nothing quite as delightful after a seemingly interminable winter than being greeted by bright cheerful flowers, with their inherent promise of spring, peeking through melting snow. The desire, perhaps need, to surround ourselves with color during the few months that our landscape isn't blanketed in white is a compelling reason to tackle the challenges of far northern gardening. The incredibly low angle of northern sunlight, which can be used to advantage for unusual and stunning effects by those who seize the challenge, is another. Majestic mountains, glittering seas, and expansive vistas offer spectacular backdrops for our garden creations. Add the magic ingredient of mild, nearly endless days during the growing season and you have a formula for spectacular, unparalleled results.

If you are an Alaskan, this book will reveal how you can take advantage of our extraordinary environment. If you're a visitor interested in Alaska, I hope you'll include our gardens as part of what you find special about this great land. And if you're a gardener from anywhere else in the world, especially another cold climate, I trust you'll find the way we garden not only interesting but also informative and useful.

There are many ways to develop a successful, productive, and beautiful garden in this vast, northernmost state. Some approaches are easier than others. My goal in this book is to present the most straightforward, surefire ways to accomplish each task, beginning with your first thoughts about creating a garden and culminating with being ready to enjoy it. By sharing what I've learned through study, experimentation, careful observation, and passionate gardening for nearly twenty years in my own Alaska gardens as well as those of my many clients, I'd like to guide you to a successful gardening experience that is rewarding and pleasurable rather than frustrating and stressful—one that is fun and joyful instead of laborious.

Woven throughout the practical advice in this book you'll find personal anecdotes and experiences, some quintessential Alaska tales (including stories of moose in the garden), in addition to customized design strategies especially suited to gardening in the Far North. Alaska is a fascinating place to visit. It's an even more fascinating place in which to live and garden. I hope *There's a Moose in My Garden* will help you capture the beguiling essence of gardening in Alaska.

Each time I've read a book, I've marveled at the number of folks who are thanked by the author. Now I understand why. Though many hours are spent in solitary, thinking and writing, what ultimately shapes a book and makes it the best it can be are the innumerable generous and thoughtful contributions of others.

My lifelong friend Jane Vandeventer played a key role in helping me get my many disparate thoughts organized so this book would flow smoothly. She also read and commented on early manuscripts. I think of her as my strategic editor. My Homer friend Roni Overway helped me break free of the habits of twenty-five years of concise business prose. I will never be able to repay her for the hours she freely gave as she read and reread draft after draft, offering insightful and detailed comments and suggestions at each stage.

I've had many wonderful mentors in my life; my Alaska gardening experience is no exception. The first were homesteaders and neighbors, the late Bob and Ann Gillas, who shared their knowledge and their plants. Then Elizabeth Shaw convinced me I had to garden here to truly understand what it meant to be an Alaskan. Rita Jo Shoultz was next. She welcomed me into her greenhouse, let me volunteer, and while we worked side by side for hours on end became my close friend and taught me her techniques and tricks. She was also instrumental in convincing me—actually, she pushed me pretty darn hard—to start a garden consultation and design business. That in turn has brought me other joys—new friends and wonderful experiences that helped inform this book.

A special thank you goes to all of my many clients who invited me to work with them to design and create the gardens they envisioned. I appreciate the trust they placed in me while giving me the pleasure of helping to create something of beauty. Thanks especially to Gari and Len Sisk, Kathy and Mike Pate, Tom Taffe and Devony Lehner, Cameale Johnson, Marguerite and Flip Felton, Denice and Roger Clyne, Cathy and Scott Ulmer, Mary and Emmitt Trimble, Marilyn and Willie Morris, Jody Murdock, Dorothy and Bill Fry, Molly and Derek Stonorov, Debbie Smith, South Peninsula Hospital Auxiliary, Derotha Ferraro, Mary Bell, Friends of the Homer Public Library, Homer Animal Friends, Dr. Dots Sherwood, Mary and Karl Schneider, and Sharon and Bruce Bardwell, whose gardens appear in this book.

I was encouraged at every turn by other gardening colleagues, several of whom made significant contributions. From the Cooperative Extension Service, Julie Riley, Janice Chumley, Tom Jahns, and Steve Brown each helped me over a hurdle with their specialized knowledge or teaching. I want to add that the Cooperative Extension Service is an organization that truly lives up to its name and ideals. Dr. Patricia Holloway, director of the Georgeson Botanical Garden and a professor of horticulture at the University of Alaska Fairbanks, twice read my manuscript for technical accuracy and completeness. Her rigorous review, meticulous suggestions, and ardent support were critical to the success of this venture.

Many well-known, successful authors freely shared their experiences and guidance in unraveling the mysteries of the publishing process. A special thank you to Cole Burrell, who offered to write a foreword for me. He spent many hours reading this book, understood its mission well, and wrote a gracious and enthusiastic foreword. He and gardening friends Tracy DiSabato-Aust, Stephanie Cohen, Erica Glasener, and Verna Pratt as well as longtime friend and incredibly amusing man Ed McManus all gave me important insight and support.

Former garden blogger and good friend Fran Durner made several key recommendations as did garden club buddy Pam Voeller. Thanks also to Teena Garay, Kim Smith, Bridget Kuhns, Peter and Flo Larson, Jenny Carroll, and Jessica Ryan for welcoming me into their lovely gardens and permitting me to take photographs. All the folks at the University of Alaska Press have been delightful to work with and have offered encouragement and assistance, especially marketing manager Amy Simpson, production editor Sue Mitchell, designer Paula Elmes, and acquisitions editor James Engelhardt. The knowledge, professionalism, and enthusiasm for this project that James provided made my transition from writer to published author much smoother and less stressful than I imagined.

My husband, the handsome man who has shared the adventures of my adult life and who provides the warm, loving environment in which I work, has also read and reread my manuscript. His sage advice and keen eye in evaluating photographs have been invaluable. He also gets me untangled when the computer doesn't do what I want it to do and is my unflinchingly loyal one-man cheerleading squad. Thank you, Willie. And thank you all. This is your book too.

## You *Garden* in *Alaska*?!

sn't it too dark in Alaska to grow flowers?" an acquaintance from Outside asked me one day. (*Outside* is what we Alaskans call everywhere else.) There are many variations of this question. Isn't it too cold? Isn't there too much snow? Aren't the summers too short? Isn't it too far north? It always surprises me how many misconceptions there are about Alaska, even among otherwise well-informed people. Perhaps these misconceptions are born of Alaska being so remote and far away. Or maybe the frigid images from Jack London's stories created unshakable impressions on our youthful minds. Whatever the reasons, many visitors, including guests in our home, are often astonished to learn we actually do garden here. News stories about the gigantic cabbages and pumpkins that win prizes at the Alaska State Fair are familiar to many people Outside, yet for some reason they do not associate brilliant flowers with Alaska—that is, until they arrive here. Or, to be more precise, until they arrive between mid-May and the end of September.

As some of you may have experienced the first time you visited Alaska or when you returned home from a trip Outside, the slow descent of a commercial flight into Anchorage (the most common entry point for visitors arriving by plane) takes you over a spectacular range of snow-covered mountains. If you are lucky enough to have a window seat and a clear day, your view is of steep, jagged, often snow-covered rocky mountaintops separated by glacier-filled valleys. This beautiful but stark scene can't possibly prepare you for the brilliant displays of flowers that greet you as you leave the airport during our summer season.

Anchorage does a fabulous job of showing off the intense colors and lush habit of our long-blooming plants. Along the streets of the downtown shopping district you'll find hanging baskets overflowing with sapphire-blue lobelia and golden marigolds representing the colors of our state flag. Surrounding the charming log cabin that houses the Visitor Information Center is an exuberant and colorful cottage garden. The small urban park known as Town Square that adjoins the Alaska Center for the Performing Arts is dressed each season in the more formal floral finery of

Alaska is famous for its glorious cabbages but less so for its incredible flowering plants.

masses of bedding plants. Each of Anchorage's public gardens is individually designed and cared for by a specific person or team from the city's Department of Parks and Recreation. This approach provides a continuity of responsibility that instills a real sense of pride in the staff, and it is evident in the results. The number, variety, and beauty of public and private gardens visible on even a brief stroll around the city will astound and inspire you.

Once we Alaskans or our guests venture onto the highways, we are greeted by profuse displays of wildflowers. Brilliant colors cover vast stretches of the mountainsides and meadows. We see the distinctive, startling, almost electric fuchsia of common fireweed or the cool purple-blue tones of wild lupine. Soft yellow paintbrush and bright yellow cinquefoil line the roadways. Moisture-loving flowers inhabit the boggy lowlands. There we see the light pink blooms of bog rosemary, aromatic drifts of the delicate-looking white flowers of Labrador tea, and the charming puffy balls of a

Exuberant gardens welcome tourists to the Visitor Information Center in downtown Anchorage.

native sedge known locally as tufted white cotton grass. Alaska's wildflowers combine with our spectacular geography to form a rich tapestry of visual delights.

Because Alaska's native plants offer such diversity, some Alaska gardeners choose to create gardens by simply encouraging some wild plant varieties on their property while keeping others in check. More often, however, Alaska gardeners incorporate a few of the natives into their gardens but also depend on the huge variety of annuals, perennials, grasses, ferns, trees, shrubs, and bulbs that are available from local nurseries to fashion their landscapes.

Clockwise:

Many gardeners invite beautiful native lupine (*Lupinus arcticus*) into their gardens.

A charming and colorful fall vignette of native plants. (Photo courtesy of Christine Wickham.)

Fuzzy Alaska cotton grass (*Eriophorum brachyantherum*) adds a whimsical note to roadside ditches.

The experiments and experiences of our pioneers have produced a body of knowledge about which plants are rugged enough to thrive here. This knowledge, along with many of these dependable stalwarts, was routinely passed from one gardener to another. I have some wonderful culinary rhubarb given to my husband, Bill, and me more than twenty years ago by our neighboring homesteaders, the late Bob and Ann Gillas. We had just moved into our home when Bob came trundling down our driveway atop his scarred and rusted old red tractor with its front bucket packed full of rhubarb plants meant to welcome us to the neighborhood. He had scooped them out of the field where he and Ann had grown rhubarb for market for years. Their plants had come from yet an earlier pioneer and we in turn have passed some divides on to Bear Creek Winery, where this nutritious food crop now also serves as an ingredient in locally produced wines. And so on it goes.

Our wonderful neighbors, the late Ann and Bob Gillas, in front of the cabin they built on their homestead.

Another pioneering Alaskan, the late Lenore Hedla, wrote extensively about gardening in our state. Lenore's book, *The Alaska Gardener's Handbook* (1994), describes many dependable, hardy plants. It is concise and instructive and I heartily recommend it. Although her books have served as reliable guides for new Alaska gardeners for many years, it has been a long time since Lenore wrote them. My purpose here is to build on her work, offer an enhanced perspective developed over the last twenty years, and broaden the dialogue to speak more to the planning and design of, preparation for, and construction of new gardens. I will also provide you with descriptions of some of my favorite plants and insight into why I value them from a designer's viewpoint.

Those of us newer to gardening in a northern climate owe our pioneers a great debt of gratitude. But just as the pioneers experimented, so do modern-day Alaska gardeners. The result is that today there is an extensive collection of proven plants from which to choose. From my experience over numerous years I've gradually created a database of more than seventeen hundred varieties of herbaceous perennials, trees, and shrubs that are hardy and successfully grown in many parts of Alaska. Bulbs, grasses, ferns, and annuals provide even more options.

❋ ❋ ❋

Alaska is an immense state. It's hard to appreciate how big it is until you climb into a car or motor home and start driving. Because it is enormous and so geographically diverse, questions about the average temperature, hours of daylight, rainfall, and topography cannot be answered meaningfully about Alaska as a whole. Neither can questions about plant zones, precipitation, or snow cover. Even in a little town the size of Homer, near my home, with a population of just over five thousand, there is seldom only one simple answer to questions of this sort. When someone asks you if a specific plant will be hardy for them (that is, tough enough to withstand the long, cold winter where they garden), you must know the altitude of their garden, the distance from the sea, the amount and dependability of snowfall, the proximity to mountains and/or glaciers, and the direction of the prevailing wind in order to answer the question precisely. We have so many microclimates, even on one plot of ground, that there are few hard and fast rules. Plants that may be successful on the south side of your home, where they benefit from gentle onshore breezes, may be scorched and wilted by the long hours of warm afternoon sun on the west side or desiccated by drying winter winds on the north side. I'll provide you with guidance on how to sort through these variables as they might relate to the circumstances of your land in Chapter 6, "Selecting Successful Plants."

Even though it may be difficult to generalize about some of the local specifics of gardening in Alaska, nearly all of us share the most compelling overall environmental factors. One that is fairly universal (except in the extreme southeast of Alaska) is a short growing season with days that are much, much longer than in the contiguous forty-eight states. This causes countless plants in their rush to create seeds to behave as if they are on high doses of powerful steroids. Things just grow bigger, faster! One summer, when my then-nine-year-old grandson Cameron visited from Texas, I took a picture of him standing next to what we call pushki. It is an indigenous plant more commonly known Outside as cow parsnip (*Heracleum maximum*) and looks like a gigantic Queen Anne's lace. In the first photo of my grandson, the pushki was just emerging from the ground. Every two days, Cameron stood next to the plant and I took another photo of him from a fixed location. It was like a scene from *Little Shop of Horrors*—within three weeks the plant towered over his head!

Many areas of New England and the northern Midwest have harsher climates than much of Alaska, but none have our incredibly long summer days. This difference may

A profusion of pale-yellow flowers decorates an Asiatic lily.

cause a plant that is hardy in North Dakota or Minnesota to do poorly even at much milder temperatures here. Sensitivity to lengthy periods of light or a biological clock that does not recognize the rapid onslaught of winter imperils some species. They are seduced by the long days in September and don't prepare for frost soon enough. But the plants that do succeed in Alaska do so with gusto.

One of the benefits of our extensive hours of daylight, especially when combined with relatively cool summer temperatures and, in coastal gardens, abundant rainfall, is how lush and floriferous it makes our perennials. I've seen a single two-year-old Himalayan blue poppy (*Meconopsis betonicifolia*) produce more than sixty-two ice-blue flowers at one time. A pale yellow Asiatic lily yielded twenty-three huge blossoms the first year it was in the ground. Many plants burst out of dormancy to enchant and amaze us with the profusion of their blooms, and because our summer temperatures are so mild, flowers are incredibly vibrant, vigorous, and long-lasting—one of the undeniable pleasures of gardening here.

Another universal challenge for all Alaska gardeners is to understand the intensity of plant growth. This is critical when you plan an Alaska garden. Plants you may have

known well in a different climate and different latitude will behave in unexpected ways. Those that thrive on heat may languish in the cold soil of spring and never mature to the point of producing flowers or seeds. Yarrow that might stand very upright and sturdy in Colorado can, especially if overfertilized, grow so big and tall in Alaska that it may flop over onto its neighbors. Allowing enough room for the exuberant growth of our successful plants is a design challenge. In early spring the garden seems sparse. By August it is topsy-turvy with plants overflowing their spaces and spilling onto each other. If you want an orderly, controlled formal garden, you will have to work very hard at it in Alaska.

The corollary to our short but intense growing season is an incredibly long dormant season. The sheer length of the winter creates additional stress on plants. Combined with extremely cold temperatures and drying winds, winter can desiccate woody plants beyond recovery. Determining which plants can tolerate these conditions and learning how to help them flourish is part of an Alaska gardener's challenge.

Alaska is a wild place in which animals roam freely. Moose wander through our land during the winter, feasting on trees and shrubs as they go. They also enjoy a taste of tulips each spring and stop during the summer to see what's on the garden menu. Bears, rabbits, porcupines, hares, voles—from the largest to the smallest creatures, all have their favorites in our gardens and take their share.

Alaska weather can be as cantankerous and unpredictable as the moose, leaving us at times with no snow cover in frigid January or a four-foot blizzard in March. When spring will *really* arrive is always a mystery from one year to the next. And then, every so often a local volcano erupts and spews ash over everything, coating flowers, foliage, mulch, and soil in powdery gray ash. Now that is definitely humbling! It's also one of the experiences we all share if we garden here long enough.

On a brighter note, even sunshine is a different experience in far northern latitudes. Our sun rides low in the sky and offers us opportunities to use light in new and different ways. We can use protracted sunrises and sunsets to visually set our gardens aglow. The low angle of the sun enables us to grow many shade plants right out in the open, thus further broadening our design possibilities. It also makes colors *look* different here than they do in locations with strong midday overhead sunshine. In the Far North jewel tones seem more saturated; pastels appear brighter; whites are radiant.

All of these factors combine to make our region of the world and our gardens unique. Gardening here is a very special journey, one filled with incomparable joys, pleasures, and experiences.

Moose looking for a garden snack stand near a seven-foot-tall arbor of alder twigs.

# Designing a Northern Garden

A young bull moose in profile with his long bell and lumpy snout rests on our deck.

Spring is a magical time in Alaska. Winter is finally a memory. Days dawn bright and crisp; they are long and succulent, filled with promise. You can almost taste the change in the air. Early bulbs peek through the waning snow. And moose return to our gardens.

In my view, a full-grown moose is an incredibly unfortunate-looking animal. Photos rarely capture how homely they actually are. I can't help but think that this might be the way a horse would appear reflected in a fun-house mirror; everything is a bit out of whack! The muzzle of a moose seems too long and broad at the tip; in profile it appears afflicted with a severe overbite. In fact, the expanded proboscis is an evolutionary novelty unique within the deer family of which moose are members.

Adding to their overall homeliness is that strange and shaggy bit of skin and hair that hangs down below their lower jaw. It's known as a *bell* or *dewlap*, but there doesn't seem to be a consensus as to its purpose. Where their necks meet their backs they have a Quasimodo-like hump. From nose to shoulders they look enormous—and they are. Then suddenly, like a hatchback car, the moose body seems to end a bit too abruptly. The back end is wanting; the tail a mere three-inch stub. Evolution has made them successful in cold and snowy climates, but it certainly hasn't made them attractive.

On the other hand, their calves are among the cutest creatures I've ever seen, with their lanky, wobbly legs and precious little faces. Their short manes stand up along their necks like a zebra's. We've seen many calves on our land within days of their birth and each experience brings a thrill of excitement and a dash for the camera. I can spend hours gazing out the windows at moose babies. The new calves are curious and playful. Holding their ears forward as they swivel their heads all around, they take in their new surroundings. Tentatively, they venture away from their mothers but canter back quickly when startled. They can be quite demanding when hungry, poking and prodding their moms insistently when they want milk. As they mature, their noses will grow and take on the lumpy attributes of their bizarre, goofy-looking mothers, but in their youth they look and act more like frisky, long-legged colts.

The cow moose that visit us in spring are heavy and swollen with the calves they are about to birth. They grunt as they amble along, emitting an "uungh" with each step. They sound as if they are terribly uncomfortable. Is this the result of moose labor pains? Perhaps.

After the long winter the moose are extremely hungry and chomp on nearly everything fresh and green that they encounter, so this is a particularly vulnerable time for our gardens. In addition to the damage their browsing causes, their huge,

sharp-hoofed feet sink deeply into the soil, which has been made soggy and soft by melting snow. The plants they trample are totally crushed and unlikely to put on a good display later even if they survive the tread of such an enormous animal.

Moose in Alaska are unavoidable in spring as many move from higher altitudes and forests to populated areas to deliver their calves. In the wilderness they must contend with predators like bears, wolves, coyotes, and wolverines; near people it's just us and our noisy dogs that trouble them.

Soon after birth the calves begin to experiment in the garden. Their mothers have already taught them that gardens are worthwhile destinations, but unfortunately, young moose don't know anything about the lists of plants that "moose eat last" so they try a taste of nearly everything. Much as we enjoy the calves, it is very frustrating to watch them tear a long branch from a tree or shrub, mouth it a little, and then spit it out. We watched as one young male bit off the entire top of one of my weeping pea shrubs (*Caragana arborescens* 'Pendula') just above the graft. Then he spit it out and moved on to the second one in the grouping. With this one, the dear boy grabbed and yanked the top, stripping part of the bark halfway down the trunk. And, yes, he spit that out too. Fortunately, by the time he reached the third, he'd figured out that these thorny shrubs were not to his liking.

When the calves gain strength and agility, their mothers lead them away from my garden and ultimately to higher ground. I'm instantly relieved, but I know that in the fall they'll be back.

I will explain the most reliable ways you can keep these special creatures out of your garden later, but first let's get started on *creating* your garden.

Note for folks from outside moose territory: Please remember that venturing too close to get a really good look at or a photograph of a moose calf can be a dangerous enterprise. Moose are shockingly fast and the mothers are extremely protective of their young. Their hooves are deadly weapons. Moose have been known to stomp people to death, so a little caution is definitely warranted.

A client's gazebo furnishes a
sheltered location to enjoy the
garden and smoke a cigar.

I f you would like to participate in the thrill of an Alaska or Far North gardening experience, you might wonder how to get started. Many books on gardening, and particularly on garden design, tell you to begin with an inventory of your site (which we'll discuss in the next chapter), but I'd like to encourage you to start more simply.

Sit down and ask yourself *why* you are thinking about creating a garden. What do you want to get out of it for *you*? What are your personal goals? Where does a garden fit among the other priorities in your life? There are no right or wrong answers, but your answers will be important in planning your garden.

There are both practical and aesthetic reasons you may want a garden or new landscape. Perhaps you want to give your home or business more curb appeal, create a retreat to enjoy at the end of a busy workday, or dedicate a place to grow food for your family. Other family members may have needs or wishes for the garden too. Do you need a play area for your children, a place for pets to exercise, a fire pit or outdoor eating area where you can entertain family and friends? Maybe you simply desire a prettier view from your kitchen, bedroom, or living room window. Because we have so many summer guests in Alaska, a hideaway to which you can retreat and be alone for a time may be desirable. In a practical sense, you may be concerned about wildfires and wish to push the existing tangle of native plant growth farther away from your home or other structures.

If you live in an area with frequent rainfall, a covered area for viewing your prospective garden or the beautiful scenery around you might be pleasurable. Would a gazebo or covered patio make sense? One of my clients wanted a gazebo with a fire ring inside it so her husband would have a warm, dry, and inviting place *outside* the house to enjoy his cigars.

Then again, there may be more esoteric reasons for you to create a garden. Do you enjoy nurturing things? Perhaps you see a garden as a way to get exercise and improve your fitness. Would you like to experience the immense satisfaction of creating something gorgeous and magical? Are you seeking an activity that will totally absorb your mind as well as your energy? A garden can be so many things; it can satisfy your desire to learn and provide a place to teach your children as well.

Each of you will have a different list, and there are many other reasons you might be contemplating a garden. The important thing is to really think about this and answer the questions for *you*. Not for someone else. You. Gardening in the far northern latitudes is not a trivial pursuit. Every garden is unique and so is every gardener.

Knowing why you want a garden is as important as knowing what you plan to create. I think this knowledge will help you to be more satisfied with the results of your efforts.

Another important question to pose to yourself is how much time you're willing or able to devote to this project, both up front and over time. When you think about this, be honest with yourself. How much time do you actually have to spend on this endeavor? What other activities and responsibilities in your life will you need to balance with the time you dedicate to your garden? As you know, gardening season is also our busy season for everything else. It's when guests come to stay, when we want to go fishing, when we build an addition onto the house. Many Alaska jobs have longer hours during the gardening season because of the tourist-driven nature of much of our commerce. You must remember that there is no such thing as a "maintenance-free" garden. We'll talk about ways to make gardens low, or rather lower, maintenance, but all gardens need some attention and care to be successful and attractive.

If you plan to tend your garden yourself and you are new to gardening or new to gardening in Alaska, my fervent advice is to start small. It is much more satisfying to have an exquisite small garden than an out-of-control large one. If a garden is too much for you to manage, it will quickly become a burden instead of a pleasure. No matter what your answers are to the questions above about why you are setting out to create a garden, I strongly doubt one of your answers will be to generate additional stress in your life. So don't. Start small and see if you like caring for a garden. If you've gardened Outside and know gardening brings you pleasure, my counsel is still to start small until you learn how vigorously plants and weeds flourish during our long days of spring and summer sunshine. If you want a larger garden than you have the time or inclination to care for, another option is to hire a knowledgeable person or maintenance firm to care for it for you.

By the way, when I use the term *garden* or *landscape*, I'm referring to the entire area outside of your home or business that you plan to enhance. Within the overall garden space there will be planted areas that I'll call *garden beds*.

Once you have your answers to the questions about your motivations and goals firmly in mind, you're ready for the next step. Study your land. Watch and record which areas receive sun and for how many hours per day during each month of the growing season. Because of the way our sun pattern moves *around* the sky rather than over it, you'll see dramatic differences from one month to the next. You should also learn the direction, frequency, and variability of wind on your property. See if there are protected areas that are less windy. Fences and buildings can cause eddies. Stone and concrete will absorb heat during the day and radiate it at night, providing special pockets of warmth. Make notes of your observations in a notebook to serve as your garden journal, a personal reference you can build over time. This information will be invaluable to you as you select plants for your garden.

In spring, note where the snow melts first and where it melts last. See if your soil drains well or if puddles persist long after the snow is gone. Dig down six inches or more and see if the soil is saturated at that depth. If you plan to add trees to your landscape, you will want to dig down two feet to check on drainage. In many areas the water table is very close to the surface for much of the year. Note which plants are currently growing where you're considering placing your garden beds since some indigenous plants, like alder, enhance the quality of soil. Some weeds are harder to eradicate than others. The important thing is to make careful, accurate observations and add them to your journal. These will help you lay out the best master plan you can before you begin digging and planting.

You may find these items helpful in creating your plans: a roll of tracing paper, quarter-inch graph paper, templates, pencils, a good eraser, and some tape to hold your layers in place. Something to help you draw curves will also be useful.

t's probably a good idea to define what I mean by a master plan. It is a description of your ultimate goal for your landscaped area—that is, for your garden. It details the main elements, including decks, walkways, and planting areas, that will be included and it delineates their locations. It shows the placement of existing structures and view corridors. If you already have garden beds that you will keep as they are or plan to enhance, include them in your master plan. All this can be done to some extent in words, but it's much more useful to sketch it out. With a drawing, even a rudimentary one, you can see how the major elements will relate to one another and where you'll need paths and entrances to draw people from one area to another and to make their transit through the garden seem natural and effortless. This is often referred to as garden "flow."

Create a scale drawing of your home or business, including all the existing fixed structures like driveways, retaining walls, utility poles, and so on. You may already have a document called an as-built survey from your builder or the borough that details all of the structures and easements on your property. If so, it will make the task of creating your scale drawing easier, as many of the dimensions you will need may be included on that document. Put your drawing on quarter-inch graph paper, using

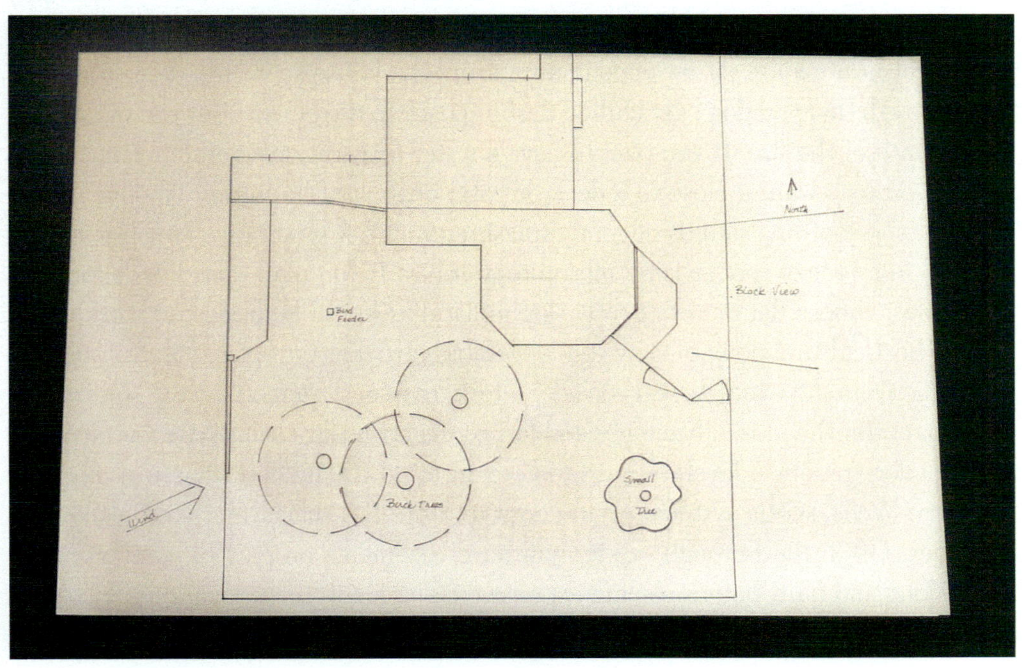

Include existing structures and trees in your base plan.

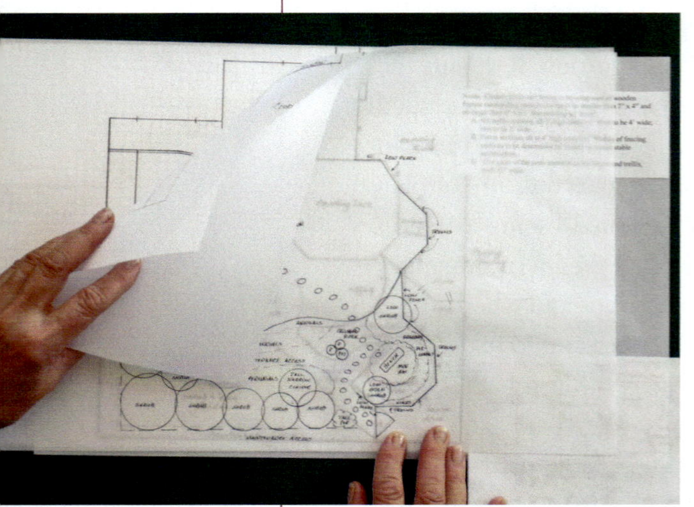

When you're satisfied with each area of your plan, add another layer of tracing paper to continue the process of refinement so you don't have to keep redrawing the parts you've completed.

each square to represent one foot. (If your property is large you may need to use each square to represent five feet or more.) Make note of views you wish to enhance and views you'd rather obscure. Indicate wind direction and the direction of north. This scale drawing will be your base drawing, your starting point. Some refer to it as a *site inventory*.

I find brainstorming and designing in layers of paper to be very helpful. To do this lay tracing paper over your base drawing and tape it in place with masking tape. You are now ready to begin trying different ideas. I suggest you start with big bold strokes designating *areas* rather than details, until you have a flow that works well. Don't be discouraged if your first attempt doesn't please you. Just replace the tracing paper with a new sheet and try again. Often it takes many attempts to come up with what you perceive to be an ideal layout.

How do you decide what to put where? To a large extent the answer to this question will be driven by your reasons for the garden. With my clients, I approach this by asking them to talk through how they'll use each element and how often. For example, serious cooks will want the herb garden near the kitchen since they'll use it daily. You might locate a fire pit far enough away from the house so it's not dangerous, but close enough that you don't get chilled dashing back to the house after you've enjoyed the warmth of the fire. If you plan to have a water feature—a fountain, waterfall, or pond—you may want it close to a deck or patio or to your bedroom window, so you can hear the soothing sounds of gently splashing water. A meditative bench might be situated in a breezy spot to keep mosquitoes at bay. If you plan raised beds for your vegetables, choose flat or very gently sloping land as it will be easiest to work upon. From a horticultural point of view your vegetable garden is best placed in full sun and protected from the wind. As you consider alternatives and tradeoffs, try to select locations that offer the most advantages and fewest negatives for each particular element.

On a very practical level, be sure to keep in mind the hidden structures on your property. Wells, septic systems, or underground utilities may affect your placement decisions. Often the borough or city will have easements on part of your property. Think long and hard before placing expensive elements in these locations. Also take note of overhead utilities. The power company will top your trees if they grow to a size that might interfere with overhead wires.

Beauty and views will likely play a key role in your placement decisions, as you'll want to draw attention to your special vistas and divert it from undesirable aspects. An alder patch that you might plan to clear to open a particular panorama should offer humus-rich soil for an ornamental garden bed, which would in turn draw attention toward the exceptional scene. A south-facing slope will provide a longer growing season than a north-facing one, as the sun will melt the snow and warm the soil much earlier. All of these factors will be influenced by the decisions you made when you held the conversation with yourself about why you were setting out on this adventure. They will also be tempered by the realities of your site.

Look at your property from inside your home. Consider locating your plantings so you'll have an attractive view from the rooms you use most often. Walk your property while you think of the different elements you want. Sometimes the lay of the land will help guide you. Locate the obvious garden elements first, and then fill in the others. Draw in paths and entrances to connect and define your various spaces. If you have enough room, design paths wide enough for two people to walk side-by-side (about four and a half feet). Wide paths will allow you to comfortably share the experience of strolling through your garden and will create a very welcoming feeling. On the other hand, there may be instances when a narrow, nearly hidden path, which can impart a sense of mystery and allure, may be better suited to achieve the effect you desire.

Transitions are a very important part of making an overall plan work. Give thought to how you and your guests will move from one area to the next. Gates, arbors, steps, paths, and the like will help you define transitions from one part of your garden to another.

## Design Software

For those who enjoy working with computers, you may prefer to do your master plan using one of the many landscape-design software packages. Though somewhat time-consuming to master, these are very useful in drawing, replicating items on the plan, and calculating material requirements. Most include a database of plants. Nonetheless, there are several reasons I suggest creating your plan by hand rather than with design software:

1. If you're planning to create just your own garden, the time to decide which package to buy and then to learn to use it seems too great a burden.

2. In all the packages I've reviewed, the bloom times cited for each plant are based on Lower Forty-Eight conditions and therefore woefully inaccurate for Alaska.

3. Few of the plants in the design software databases are hardy enough for Alaska.

4. *Keep it simple* has always been my motto.

All other things being equal, a south-facing slope provides a longer growing season.

As you put these pieces together to form your master plan, feel free to tear up several attempts until you get a plan that you think flows well. If you get frustrated it helps to walk away from the plan for a day or two and then come back with a new sense of optimism and purpose. I find I get some great breakthrough ideas during a good night's sleep. Really!

This is a good time to think about the overall style of your garden and the type of materials you'll use for paths, fences, and the like. Style refers to the look of your landscape. For example, it might be very informal using curving paths of natural stone or crushed rock and full, lush garden beds with a riot of mixed colors. This works well with many Alaska homes, especially log or cedar ones. An approach at the opposite end of the spectrum is a more formal look using straight lines, manufactured masonry, and symmetrical features with a monochromatic design for the plantings. If your home is quite elegant or very modern, this could be a good direction for you. There are many approaches to take between these two extremes, but matching the style of your garden to the style of your home and the way you plan to enjoy your garden and its surroundings will help you create an environment that feels right to you.

In addition to style there are other things to think about as you design your garden. One is scale—what size major items in the garden such as trees, garden beds, and art pieces need to be to look their best. The dimensions of your home, particularly its height, should influence your decisions about this aspect of your design. There are a variety of guidelines on this topic. For example, the width of a garden bed should be approximately one-third the height of the background. Plants should be one-half to two-thirds as high as the background. So, if your home is twenty feet high, a garden along its façade would be about seven feet wide with some trees or shrubs ten to fourteen feet high.

A famous ratio used for millennia, the golden ratio or golden mean, offers us similar guidance when creating a harmonious composition that looks in balance. The actual ratio is 1 to 1.618 or roughly two to three. Following this guideline, a twenty-one-foot-long garden bed would be about fourteen feet wide. An important focal point will feel well placed if located two-thirds of the way from one end of the garden bed, one-third from the other. It's neither always possible nor desirable to follow guiding principles like these to the letter, but they do provide a starting point for your consideration.

As important as the size of your home is in determining scale, the overall environment of your location also plays a role. In Alaska our vistas are often immeasurable as well as beautiful. Our mountains are imposing, most native trees are tall, and many of us enjoy sizable properties compared to those Outside. Simply put, the elements of our environment are big! How should this influence your decisions about scale?

Traditional design guidance would dictate a very substantial garden to stand up to the imposing features around it. However, few of us have the time or inclination to manage an enormous one. So, without attempting to landscape a gigantic area, how do you make your gardening efforts command attention? One answer is to be bold in your choices. Use big rocks instead of small ones, one dramatic piece of garden art instead of several less compelling ones. You'll get more impact from tall plants, deep garden beds, and broad paths. Another approach is to keep the garden close to you and your primary viewing location. The closer it is, the larger it looks and the more visual impact it will have.

You can use visual tricks to make your garden appear more expansive than it is. A favorite approach of mine is to "borrow a view." For example, if you have a field of fireweed on your property, you can use it as a backdrop for a garden bed in which you incorporate some plants of the same fuchsia color. The color repetition will visually tie the two together. If you have a magnificent vista, frame it with some trees or tall shrubs. This technique will make the view seem an integral part of your garden. Use spruce or alder that is already on-site as part of the background, thus incorporating it into your tableau. All of these approaches will increase the overall presence and impact of your garden.

To imbue your garden with a sense of unity and cohesiveness you can select a distinct material to use throughout. For example, this could be slate paths or

Vast panoramas of mountains and glaciers can make scale a challenge.

rusted-metal art pieces. If you plan several arbors, use similar styles or the same material in each. Edging all your garden beds in a consistent way can achieve this as well. You can also use repetition of color to hold a garden together. Some gardeners use a collection of frogs, garden gnomes, personal mementos, or other forms of garden art as a theme that successfully brings unity to their garden. There is no need to be overly regimented about this concept, but reiteration of some kind will add an element of cohesiveness. The same principle works within the garden beds as well. Repeating a color, plant, form, or combination will help move the viewer's eye through your garden bed and make the design coalesce.

One of the critical decisions you'll have to make is whether or not you'll fence your garden to try to keep moose and other critters out. Will you fence all of it, just certain sections, or none of it? Think about snow removal and plow access if you do decide to use fencing. One of my friends thought a cattle guard on the driveway of her otherwise fenced yard would keep moose at bay, but it turns out moose are a lot smarter than cows. On the very first day that snow and ice filled the cattle guard, the moose walked right over it into the garden and began devouring her shrubs! Fences are expensive and not foolproof, but if high and sturdy enough, they can give you a lot more freedom in your plant selections.

If your garden will be a multiyear project, and in our do-it-yourself tradition many Alaska gardens are, your drawing will help make clear which parts are most logical to construct first. It's pretty frustrating to realize after the fact that an element you just implemented blocks access for the heavy equipment you may need for a future phase. A Bobcat can save you an enormous amount of labor, but only if you can get it to the place you need to use it. When we install a garden for a client, especially in a multiyear plan, we like to do as many of the structural items, also called hardscape, as the budget allows during the first year. If the budget requires us to split the work over more than one year, we like to start working at the farthest point from the road. With this approach we can avoid running heavy equipment over areas that have been completed while implementing the next phase.

Regardless of the size of your project or whether it is complex or simple, starting the process by putting your thoughts and concepts on paper will help you see things much more clearly. This improved vision will guide you to greater success overall.

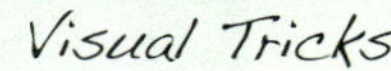

### Visual Tricks

Move things closer to increase their impact.

Borrow a view.

Frame a vista.

Incorporate larger existing trees and shrubs like spruce or alder as a backdrop.

Frame a spectacular vista like this one of the Homer Spit and distant mountains to visually connect it to your garden.

A narrow,
natural-looking
path through
this woodland
engenders a sense
of adventure
and mystery.

Hardscape is a fairly comprehensive term that refers to just about everything in the overall garden except the soil and plants. Patios, decks, the driveway, ponds and waterfalls, other water features, rocks, retaining walls, paths, bridges, fences, and structures like gazebos, pergolas, and arbors are all considered part of the hardscape. By its very definition, hardscape is an enduring and defining component of a garden. Deciding which elements to incorporate, where to place them, and how each will relate to your overall plan are vital steps in the process of creating a successful garden. The look and feel of your landscape will be strongly influenced by the choices you make regarding materials and structures. Let's examine each more closely.

## Paths

The most common hardscape element in a garden is a path. These simple structural components connect the different areas of the landscape and organize its flow. They can play a critical role in the success of your project by how effectively they draw you into the garden. While wide paths are most welcoming, a narrow, almost hidden path can be alluring for solitary explorers. In either case, a solid, level surface is most comfortable for walking.

Many different kinds of materials are useful in creating paths. Some examples used to create an informal garden are crushed rock, beach rock, natural stone, grass, or mulch. A more formal garden might incorporate manufactured stone, slate, or pavers. The material you select for your paths will be important in setting the style and feel of your garden and provide another tool to unify it. We'll discuss the advantages of different materials and how to create your paths using them in Chapter 15, "Techniques to Lower Maintenance."

The course of a garden path not only takes you from one area to another, it also influences how you experience the garden itself. A curving, meandering path will slow the passage of visitors, encouraging them to take in the details of what you've

Broad, elegant slate paths lure you into the garden and add a unifying element to the design.

Natural stepping-stones laid in gravel complement the theme of an informal rock garden.

Simple paths of beach rock are an inexpensive and utilitarian option for a cottage vegetable garden, seen here after the harvest has been completed.

## Path Facts

Wide paths are welcoming.

Narrow, partly hidden paths are alluring.

All need level, solid footing to be safe and comfortable.

Curved paths invite us to linger.

Straight paths are traversed more quickly.

worked so diligently to achieve. Straight paths are more efficient, but people tend to walk down them much more quickly. So if you want people to savor your garden, slow them down with some well-placed curves. Situating fragrant plants or a bench along the path and allowing some vegetation to spill onto the path are techniques used to reinforce the inclination to dally in your garden and extend the experience of it.

## Water Features

Another garden feature that will lure folks into your garden is a pond, an enchanting addition to any landscape. The shimmering movement and musical sound of water along with its reflective qualities are incredibly captivating. If you wish to create an environment that attracts and supports wildlife, adding a pond will also help you achieve this goal. It may surprise you to know that a large pond and a small one require about the same amount of ongoing maintenance once the pond is constructed. My recommendation is to make your pond as spacious as practical, as every benefit it will provide will be multiplied by its size. Before you embark on the construction of a water feature, I strongly suggest you read one of the many booklets that lay out the details of pond construction. These are often available at home improvement stores.

Some people who have clay soil are quite frustrated by it when planting their garden beds but benefit from it greatly when adding a water feature. In areas with extensive clay strata, ponds can be created by simply digging a hole and guiding snow-melt and rain runoff into it. Ponds of this sort can be quite extensive and virtually care for themselves. They also invite us to utilize a special group of plants called marshland

Letting plants spill onto your path adds a feeling of mystery and intimacy.

People tend to walk more quickly down a straight path.

or marginal aquatic perennials, meaning those that grow along the edges of water. Yellow flag iris (*Iris pseudacorus*), marsh marigold (*Caltha palustris*), and the bold-leaved umbrella plant (*Darmera peltata*) all do well in this environment, though umbrella plant is not as hardy as the first two.

If you're not blessed with clay soil or prefer a constant level of water in your pond, a liner of some sort will be necessary. Many building supply stores carry rigid pond liners in various shapes. These are sturdy and simple, though limited in size and difficult to camouflage well around the edges. Flexible pond liners give you more options as to shape and size but require care in their installation to preserve the integrity of the liner. Because moose regularly visit our pond in early spring, I've put a thick layer of round river rock on top of our liner to protect it from their sharp hooves. It's worked so far, but moose can be a danger to pond liners. So can the family pet. I had originally planned to give our water garden an exotic name, but after our chocolate Labrador retriever decided to swim in it daily except when frozen solid, I relented and named it "Eric's Garden" in his honor.

If you create a pond, you may also want a waterfall, stream, or fountain to complete the scene. Streams are fairly simple to build, especially if you have a slope next to your pond. If you don't already have a slope, you can create one with the soil excavated from the hole for the pond. A channel for the water course, a liner to prevent water loss, and some smooth rocks to cover the liner will do the trick. Using a variety of rock sizes and arranging them in a somewhat random fashion will make the stream more naturalistic.

Waterfalls are a bit trickier than streams and take more planning to achieve the effect you want, but they are well worth the effort. It's important to make the water channel sufficiently deep and wide to contain splashing water as it tumbles over the falls. It's amazing how much water you can lose in a twenty-four-hour period with just

Reflections shimmer even on a small pond.

A larger pond multiplies the special effects that water brings to a garden.

A cow and calf enjoy the marginal aquatic plants in this clay-bottomed pond. The calf appears to be sniffing a yellow flag iris (*Iris pseudacorus*) blossom, but it's more likely he's about to eat it! (Photo courtesy of Rita Jo Shoultz.)

## Why Use Botanical Names?

The common names of plants are often colorful and sometimes quite descriptive. The historical origins of many of these names can be fascinating. Common names are a traditional part of gardening and, for many, the only name by which a plant is known. What then is the reason for using botanical names?

Common names are not precise. Many are regional, with the same plant being called different things in different places. The plant Alaskans call pushki is referred to Outside as cow parsnip. Other common names are widely inclusive. For example, a number of distinctly different types of plants are referred to as daisies.

Botanical names, on the other hand, are unique and universal. Each plant has precisely one botanical name whether you garden in China or Alaska. Thus they transcend language barriers. Learning and using botanical names when ordering plants, especially online, will ensure that you get the specific plants you desire. To help you get used to seeing and learning botanical names and so you can search for plants pictured or discussed in specific, I will include the botanical name of a plant in parentheses following its common name. To avoid making this too burdensome for you, I'll stick with just the common names for broad groups of plants, like roses or alder.

A local cow moose and her three healthy-looking calves quickly discovered this new "moose wading pool." You can see some of the recently excavated material along the far bank. (Photo courtesy of Rita Jo Shoultz.)

Eric enjoys his pond as soon as he can break through the ice.

A small fountain splashes water under the watchful gaze of Mr. Frog.

Waterfalls add enjoyment, motion, and sound to a pond.

This is the same pond a bit later in the year. We left the pump in too long and had to break the ice to remove it!

### Additional Information on Water Features

*Garden Pools, Fountains and Waterfalls* edited by Scott Atkinson and the editors of Sunset Books (Sunset Publishing Group)

*The Complete Guide to Water Gardens, Ponds and Fountains* by Kathleen Fisher (Creative Homeowner)

*Ortho's All About Building Waterfalls, Ponds and Streams* by Ortho Books editorial staff (Ortho Books)

*Gardening with Water* by James van Sweden (Grayson Publishing)

a little splashing out. As with ponds, my counsel is to refer to books or pamphlets that address this subject in detail before tackling a waterfall.

When you've constructed your stream or waterfall, you can connect a small submersible pump to a hose to carry the water to the top of the fall or stream. You can hide the hose under a layer of soil or mulch.

The sound of your waterfall can be determined by the pump and hose capacity you choose, which in turn will increase or decrease the amount of water flow. The height of each step in the cascade and even the careful placement of rocks in the stream will affect the quality, tone, and character of the ambience created. You may choose a large volume of water to mask loud traffic noise, a gentle gurgle to simulate a meandering stream in a forest glen, or a joyous harmony to set the stage for entertainment. In any event, the music of moving water can transform your environment into an enchanted place.

A fountain of water can be created with an attachment to a submersible pump that sprays the water into the air. There are many spray patterns available, each of which will create a different visual and audible effect. There is also a variety of self-contained water fountains from a humble gurgling bubbler to an elaborate display. As you contemplate your choices, keep the style and goals of your garden in mind so your water feature fits in and looks like it belongs.

Often, when adding a water feature after home construction is completed, the most troublesome issue with making water move is a power source. Once you've solved that problem and have enjoyed your pond all season, don't forget to remove the pump before the pond ices over.

## Gazebos, Pergolas, Arbors, and Gates

Structures like gazebos, pergolas, and arbors can really add pizzazz to your garden. Their height provides vertical strength to your design in a way that's similar to well-placed trees. They also present a focal point, a destination, and a place of retreat. All are wonderful elements. Because many of us experience a lot of rainy days, I find a gazebo a very inviting and practical option because of its solid roof. Those of you who garden in the warmer, drier Interior may enjoy the shade offered by a gazebo.

Arbors and gates have a special role to play in a garden. They provide a strong visual signal to garden guests that they are entering a new, perhaps quite different area. You can use a gate, an arbor, or a combination of the two to create a sense of

Without the strength and verticality of a structure, this garden is not nearly as impactful.

The added gazebo generates more balance in the garden. Its presence serves as an invitation to enter the garden to enjoy its pleasures.

Clockwise:

A pergola with a built-in bench makes a nice destination and lures you into the garden. (Photo courtesy of Christine Wickham.)

A charming white picket fence, arbor, and gate welcome and guide visitors into a casual vegetable and flower garden.

One of the advantages of sturdy structures in your garden is that they maintain a presence throughout winter without the need for moose-proofing. Moose and even bears can be a problem with less substantial twig structures made with willow or alder.

mystery by obscuring the view of what is to come. This transition point gives you, the creator of the garden, an opportunity to make a marked change in color palette, plant selection, or overall feel on either side of it. This works especially well if you can't see beyond the arbor or gate as you approach it.

Steps are often thought of as a purely practical structure used to make the walk from one level of your property to another more comfortable, but they too can heighten anticipation of what is to come. Curving a stairway as it goes down is an effective way to accomplish this.

## Patios and Decks

Patios and decks can also be places of refuge, but because they're usually attached to your home they are visually an even more integral part of it. Though an outdoor kitchen, so popular now in warmer climates, seems impractical in most of Alaska, a patio or deck large enough for a table and chairs is a delightful place to entertain on a sunny day. Like water features, patios and decks are better when bigger. In many

An expansive deck provides room for relaxing, entertaining, and lots of flower-filled containers.

cases, these elements will already exist before the garden is built. If so, the material from which they're made may suggest (but does not need to dictate) your choice for other hardscape elements in your garden.

Consistency in your selection of hardscape materials is one way to bring a sense of unity to your landscape. If your patio is made of slate, consider using slate for your paths or, to reduce costs, slate stepping-stones set in gravel walkways. Very effective designs can be achieved with a mix-and-match approach, but be cautious when mixing natural finishes with manufactured ones as the results can be jarring.

## Retaining Walls, Terraces, and the Like

Steeply sloping properties often require consideration of retaining walls, dry-stack walls (those built without mortar), terraces, or similar items. Depending on the degree of slope and how extensive the sloping area is, you may have to look at substantial structures to control erosion and stabilize your hillside. The melting snow load, which often totally saturates our soils, and the recurring freeze and thaw process introduce

A steeply sloping area required massive rocks to stabilize it. We featured these incredible rocks by selecting subtle, understated plants for the garden. Notice the curved rock stairway "hidden" on the left side of the image.

powerful forces and dynamics. If you have steeply sloping terrain, I strongly recommend you involve someone who has structural and soil mechanics training and experience to help you properly retain your garden.

Fortunately, most properties have manageable grades that can be tamed with a few timbers, low dry-stack walls, or terraces with a few rocks tucked here and there. Again, the approach you choose will depend on the look and style you want and your budget constraints. Another alternative you might want to consider with sloping ground is a rock garden or rockery. (Without getting into all the nuances, the essential difference has to do with the soil between the rocks. Rock gardens are specialized environments created for alpines and other exotic rock garden plants. A rockery is a garden where rocks are featured among more commonplace plants. Nonetheless, most folks refer to both as rock gardens. I will too.) The stones will help hold your slope in

A small raised garden built with medium-size river cobbles and mulched with gravel creates a fast-draining environment for drought-tolerant plants.

Attractive marbled, greenish granite provides a dramatic setting for the plants in this handsome rock garden.

A large rock garden that also retains a steep slope is planted with billowy, warm-hued plants.

place and the natural drainage offered by sloping ground is an excellent environment for the majority of rock garden plants.

## Rock Gardens and Featured Rocks

Rock gardens, even created on flat ground, are an excellent option for Alaska gardeners because they drain so well, shedding water easily during our erratic spring and fall temperature swings. Like all garden features, the style of a rock garden can vary quite a bit to reflect the tastes of the person designing it. The look will differ depending on the kind and sizes of rock used as well as whether you feature the rocks themselves or focus more attention on the plants.

Rocks don't have to be in a rock garden to be an interesting part of your landscape. A single large, solitary boulder can create substantial visual appeal in a garden or garden bed. The mass and texture of stone makes an extraordinary counterpoint to the soft lushness of flowers and foliage. While not readily available in some parts of Alaska and expensive in most, a large, striking-looking rock is a coveted garden feature.

## Thoughts About Irrigation and Lighting

Two other hardscape things to ponder: (1) do you need irrigation? and (2) can you think of any reason for landscape lighting? Quite a number of folks in Anchorage and Fairbanks have installed irrigation systems and seem happy with them. Automatic sprinklers can be a time-saver as well and in our larger towns there are firms that will install, maintain, and prepare them for winter. I haven't found the need for an irrigation system as I usually water only a few times each season after a garden is established. I'm able to do this for two reasons: (1) the rainfall where I garden is usually well spaced; and (2) I make a practice of watering deeply whenever I do water. By watering deeply, you encourage root growth to go down rather than stay near the soil's surface. Shallow roots will dry out much faster during drought conditions than will deep ones. The frequency of rainfall where you garden as well as the time you are able or wish to spend watering will influence your choice regarding irrigation. I find watering by hand a meditative activity, one that offers an opportunity to examine the health and growth of each plant as I water it, but others may find it tedious or boring.

What about lighting? Is it needed in Alaska or other parts of the Far North? While the notion of an evening garden expertly lit might appear alluring in the pages of a gardening magazine, it may seem just a bit daft when the sun is still going full blast at ten o'clock at night. In winter, the garden lights are buried in snow. Landscape lighting can be wonderfully effective where the sun sets early, so perhaps those of you who garden in Southeast Alaska may want to consider it. As for me, at latitude 59, I'd rather spend that money on more plants.

The blossoms of hardy 'Rozanne' geranium (*Geranium wallichianum* 'Rozanne') dance in front of a large, solitary, mountain-shaped boulder.

This frequent garden visitor
can devour forty pounds of
twigs in a day!

The first question just about everyone new to gardening in Alaska asks is, "What do you do about the moose?" It's a good question. They will ravage a tree into a flagpole, a shrub to a nub, and a tulip to absolutely nothing. Our moose are free ranging and numerous. They roam our cities and rural areas with equal aplomb. They sleep on our decks, eat along the roadsides, and wander the parking lot at the local post office. They graze farmers' newly sprouting fields, enjoy a swim in our ponds, and they ruminate outside office windows. They are simply everywhere!

Moose eat an enormous amount of vegetation—about forty pounds per day. Much of their diet consists of the stems of woody plants, but they eat all sorts of greens and flowers as well. In summer, when their native browse is available, they generally abandon our gardens, but like most "facts" about moose, there are exceptions to this one too. Moose don't seem to know *any* of the rules governing what they eat or don't eat. If hungry enough, they'll eat anything available. A sad tale testifying to their lack of discrimination occurred in Anchorage a few winters ago. A hungry young moose ingested so much of a tree poisonous to moose that it died. (The chemical that killed the moose was cyanide, but which tree was the source of it remains unsettled.)

So what is a gardener to do? You can be philosophical and accept that no matter what ingenious barrier you devise, eventually a hungry moose will find a way to gain access to your garden and eat more in one night than you may care to imagine. That's just the way it is. It's part of gardening in this wonderful, wild place. Like it or not, we share the vegetation on our land with these huge, gangly, funny-looking but somehow elegant creatures. In return, the moose, through their antics and especially those of their young offspring, provide us special moments of joy. I think it's a fair trade, but then, I've become a *philosophical* Alaska gardener.

Let me assure you, however, I'm also a practical one. It took many years and the loss of several trees and shrubs as well as countless, obviously delicious tulips before I came up with some techniques short of a fence to thwart our hungry moose. I'll share these with you soon, but let's start with the big question: Should you fence your garden?

In moose country, this is indeed *the* question. There are many trade-offs to consider. A high, sturdy fence that completely surrounds the garden area frees you to select plants without regard to what the moose might eat. This can be wonderfully liberating and will generate fence envy among your gardening friends. If you're contemplating a fruit orchard as part of your garden, a high and stout fence is not an

option but rather an absolute necessity, at least around the orchard. Short of that, whether or not to have a fence raises economic as well as practical concerns.

Fences, especially for large areas, are expensive and they're not foolproof. A starving moose can be very creative in seeking a point of entry. If there's little snow, he'll find the one place where there's a gap along the bottom of the fence and push on it until it gives enough for him to be able to squeeze under. It's remarkable how such a large animal can wriggle through such a small space. If there's a lot of snow, the moose may use the extra elevation offered by the compacted snow to leap over the top of a fence that is otherwise deemed high enough. If you do decide to fence, take into account your maximum expected snowpack and remember to close the gate *every* time.

Unfortunately, even a closed gate is not always foolproof. At a lovely garden in Homer, a gardening friend's husband built an attractive and artistic garden entrance with sturdy curlicued metal double doors held closed by a strong locking mechanism. The doors are about seven feet high. Above them is a small space and above that is a decorative arch and cross beam. The entrance is embellished with a large ship's bell. Very early one morning my friends were awakened by the sound of the bell clanging. It turned out that a cow moose had tried to enter their garden by jumping between the gates and the arch but got stuck partway through the opening. Picture an

A snugly wrapped shrub is ready for winter.

Burlap-wrapped shrubs point toward the winter sun in perfect parallel with the roofline of the house.

eight-hundred-pound moose half into and half out of the garden, precariously balanced on the gates, flailing frantically in an effort to free herself. The big bell continued to ring loudly from all the moose motion, no doubt adding to her distress! Fortunately, the moose finally dislodged herself by sliding backwards off the gate and not into the garden. Though this moose was foiled, the story makes clear that a stout high fence will *help* protect your garden, but there are no guarantees it will keep hungry moose away from your delectable plants.

Occasionally, a fence that's high enough to keep moose out will also be just tall enough to block your view. Sometimes the configuration of your property and the driveway access may make it very difficult to create a complete enclosure. Despite the obstacles, if you are able to protect your garden with an attractive fence, by all means do so.

But if you are not able to fence your garden, don't fret—you have other options. There are myriad products on the market designed to repel deer, and a few of these claim to deter moose as well. The experience of gardeners I know is that these products work, at least for awhile, in summer and during mild winters. However, when moose are starving, they ignore sprays and fluttering objects or any other ingenious scare tactics you might have devised. They go for the food every time.

Physical barriers seem to be the more effective solution. Even among physical barriers, some are better than others. In my experience, the two most dependable techniques are (1) wrapping and tying the tree or shrub in burlap and (2) surrounding

Individual wire cages surround trees and a shrub. They are held in place by rebar stakes. Protective cages are Alaska's version of "winter interest" in the garden!

Here a cage is used to surround an entire garden bed. Each end of the cage is secured to eye bolts on the house wall.

the tree or shrub with a sturdy, well-anchored wire cage. If you wrap, be quite careful to fully secure the fabric with strong twine so the moose can't rip it off and lunch on your shrubbery. Many people get good results from wrapping with burlap. One downside, though, is that the burlap can trap more snow on top of your woody plant, adding stress to its branches. It is also very unattractive.

The second effective moose barrier is a sturdy cage for each tree or shrub or group of them. We use the heavy wire mesh normally employed to reinforce concrete because it's rigid and unyielding. To hold the cage in place, it's necessary to pound several strong stakes into the ground and lash the cage to them. Five-foot lengths of half-inch rebar work, as do metal fence T-posts. Plastic cable ties will securely hold the cage to the stakes. A more elegant approach when caging is to sink three-quarter-inch pipe two feet into the ground nearly level with the soil around the garden bed or tree clump. Then when it's time to install the cage you can just drop the rebar rods into the pipe and you won't have to pound them in each fall and pry them loose each spring.

One-inch chicken wire protects the lower part of the tree from hares while the big cage wards off the moose. You can definitely see the benefits of fencing the entire garden. This individual protection takes a lot of time in fall and spring.

A chicken-wire surround works well for conifer shrubs and clematis vines.

Another benefit of cages is that you can still see your trees and shrubs *and* enjoy their fall colors and attractive bark into the winter. The trade-off is that cages are more expensive than burlap, and the wire mesh can give your fingers a nasty pinch as you work with it. Wear gloves.

Cyclical explosions in the snowshoe hare population force gardeners to take additional winter precautions to protect their woody plants. Fine-gauge chicken wire is an effective barrier, but it also must be well anchored to keep hares out.

Some use stock fencing, which has smaller holes in the lower part and larger ones higher up, to try to keep out both rabbits and moose. This can be effective where snow depths are minimal, but if snow builds up enough the rabbits will be able to walk right through the larger holes.

Because caging and wrapping may require you to stand in the garden, wait until the ground is slightly frozen to do your installation. In spring be *very sure* the moose have moved on and hares have alternative browse available before you remove the burlap or cages.

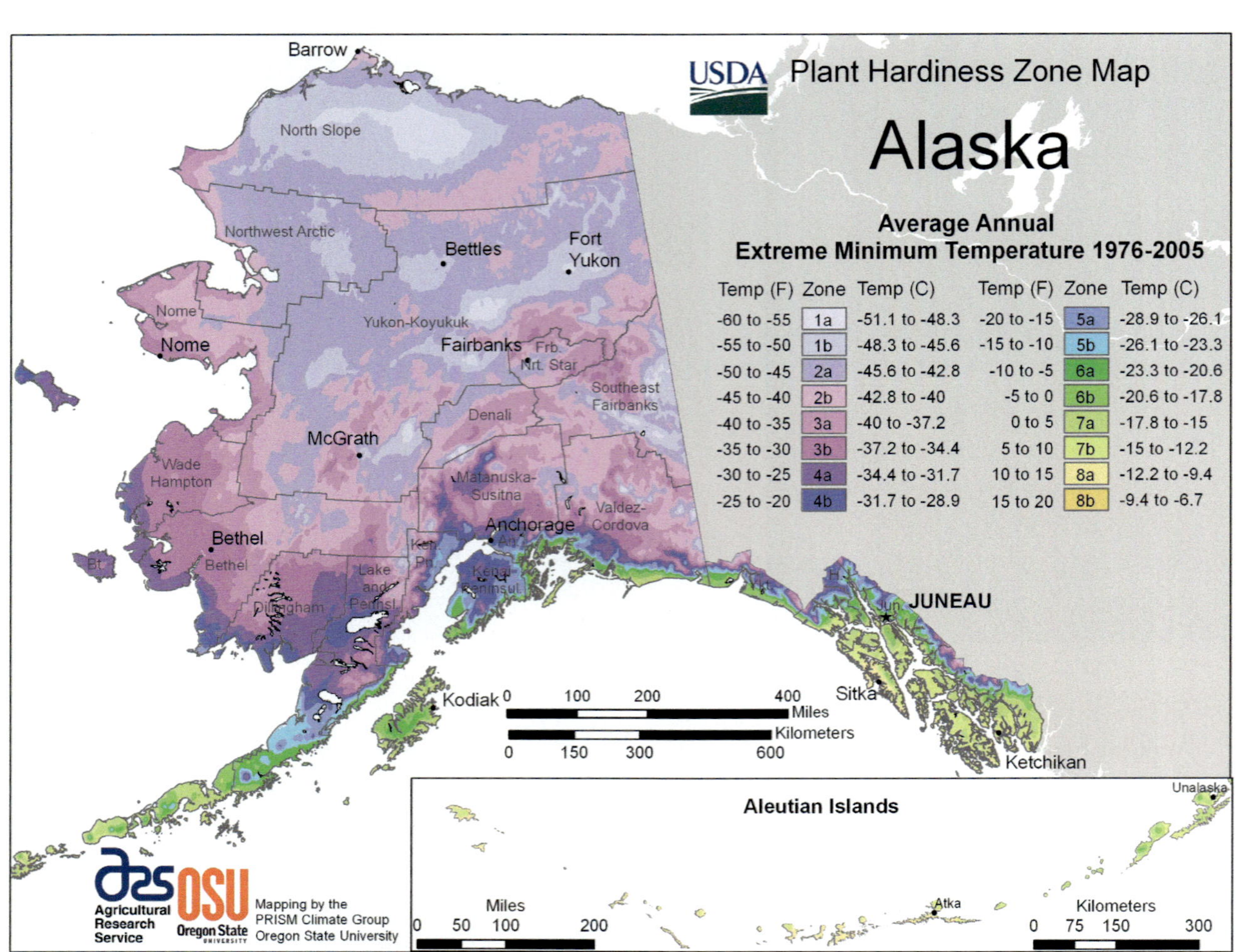


USDA Plant Hardiness Zone Map, 2012. Agricultural Research Service, U.S. Department of Agriculture. Accessed from http://planthardiness.ars.usda.gov.

# 6

When you have completed your master plan, you will be ready to focus on your plant choices. The easiest way to garden successfully anywhere is to select well-behaved plants that will flourish where you plant them. Does that seem obvious? Unfortunately, too many of us either don't learn enough about what a given plant needs for healthy growth or we choose to ignore what we do know because we want to grow it no matter what. For example, in Chapter 10, "Bark, Berries, and Fragrance," I explain why I continue to plant lavender each year, knowing it likely won't come back for me. My willingness to accept this normally perennial plant as a one-year wonder is intentional; I'm ignoring what I know. While that may be okay in a specific case, it's not a good strategy for your whole garden.

As plants evolve in their natural habitat, they develop adaptations or strategies to succeed in the set of environmental circumstances prevalent in their indigenous locations. A plant's success in your own garden will depend on how well matched your garden is to the habitat where the plant evolved, especially as regards the amount of sunlight and moisture, the type of soil, soil pH, soil fertility, and ambient temperature during both the growing season and during dormancy. Other factors—like wind exposure, humidity, day length, and length of each season—are also important. Taken together, these are known as a plant's cultural needs or requirements. Therefore, if we can understand the environment in which a plant evolved and flourished and then place it in similar circumstances, we increase our potential for success. One of the reasons that plants that are native to a specific area are so successful when invited into a local garden is that they've already adapted to that area.

Fortunately, many plants will tolerate a range of conditions that vary somewhat from their native habitat so we are able to enjoy a fairly wide range of selections beyond those of local natives. There are regions around the globe, especially at the northern latitudes, that have habitats similar to our own and from which some wonderful plants hail. In order to make good plant choices for your particular environment it's important to understand more about cultural specifics. While my goal here is to convey technical information in an easy-to-understand manner, some of what follows may seem a little eye-glazing. Nonetheless, please stick with me, because this will be a critical key to your success. So here goes.

Most cultural needs are expressed as a range or a guideline on a scale. Sunlight is a measure of how many hours of sun a plant needs per day. You'll see this described as *full sun* (six to eight or more hours of direct sun), *part sun* or *part shade* (up to six hours of direct sun so long as at least four of these are in the morning), *dappled shade* (sunlight filtered through the foliage of taller plants and trees), and *full shade* (less than three hours of sun early in the day). Full shade is generally found on the north side of a building or fence and can be challenging in Alaska, because without the benefit of warming sunshine the soil will stay cold remarkably far into the season.

In Alaska, for a perennial plant, tree, or shrub to thrive and do well through the winter it must be hardy for us. *Hardiness* is a guideline of how much cold a plant will tolerate. To express this easily, the U.S. Department of Agriculture has established and mapped a set of standard zones. Zone is a measure of average annual minimum temperatures in a given area. The range of zones in which a plant is expected to succeed describes how hardy a plant is: the lower the number, the more cold tolerant the plant will be. Simply speaking, in a northern climate, hardiness measures how much cold a plant can tolerate without protection, *provided that its other cultural needs are met.* For example, cold, drying winds can reduce a plant's ability to thrive within its zonal range, while mulch applied in winter to herbaceous perennials may protect them enough to withstand colder temperatures than they can tolerate without protection.

Much of interior Alaska is Zone 1, progressing to Zone 2 as you move closer to the sea. Along the coast, zones vary from 3 to 5, with areas in Southeast Alaska designated Zone 6 and 7 on the USDA maps. The USDA maps don't take microclimates or detailed local variances into account. They have been criticized by some as inaccurate for Alaska, but they are the best we have so far and do provide a useful starting point. Dependable winter snow cover or the lack thereof may also affect what will work for you. If you are at the beginning of your Alaska gardening experience, I suggest taking a conservative approach to zones. In other words, if the map says your area is a Zone 3, select plants that are rated Zone 3 or lower. Once you become more experienced you can experiment with a few plants at a time to see how far you can push the zone limit.

Among the most important cultural requirements for plant health is a good match between plant and soil, yet this is a frequently overlooked issue. Soil is the medium through which plants receive their sustenance, so its suitability for a given plant is vital for gardening success. Because it is difficult to dramatically or quickly change the nature of your soil, it is far easier to achieve success by learning about the soil you have and selecting plants that will thrive in it rather than the reverse—selecting plants first, then trying to change the soil to meet their needs. This second course will be fraught with disappointment. Ignoring the issue altogether is even worse.

The metrics associated with soil suitability include fertility, pH, the physical makeup of the soil, and its ability to retain water. Fertility measures the amount and kind of nutrients in the soil. Soil pH is a measure of the relative acidity or alkalinity of it and is expressed as a number from 1 (extremely acidic) to 14 (extremely alkaline) with 7 representing neutral. Physically, soil can be made up of small particles (clay), large ones (sand), or those of intermediate size (silt). Loam has an approximately equal mix of clay, sand, and silt. The amount of decayed vegetative matter as well as the particle size will affect the soil's water-retention ability.

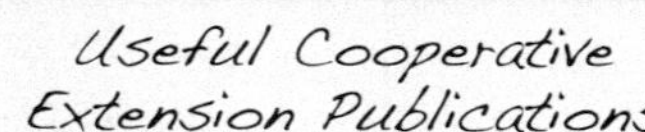



FGV-00044: Soil Sampling

FGV-00045: Factors to Consider in Selecting a Soil Test Laboratory

FGV-00043: Managing Alaska Soils

HGA-00338: Soil and Fertilizer Management for Healthy Gardens

The most dependable way to get an accurate understanding of the fertility, pH, and physical makeup of your soil and how to improve it is to have it tested. I strongly recommend that you do this. Believe me, you will be many dollars ahead in the end by beginning your gardening adventure with this step.

The University of Alaska Fairbanks (UAF) Agricultural and Forestry Experiment Station, Soil and Plant Analysis Laboratory performs soil tests for gardeners as well as agricultural growers. The results of these tests are sent directly to both the gardener and his or her local Cooperative Extension Service (CES) agent. Your agent will automatically provide an analysis of your soil test that will help you understand your starting point and will also offer guidance on what amendments are necessary for healthy plant growth. This will be in the form of a recommended fertilization and liming plan based on what you stated you plan to grow (perennials, vegetables, or lawn) in the tested area and whether you wish to employ conventional or organic methods. UAF will keep your test results on file for your future reference. This testing and analysis is available at a nominal fee—about what you might spend for three or four perennials.

There are no private labs doing soil testing in Alaska; however, there are out-of-state labs available. Though these will likely be less expensive than UAF, you will have to determine that the private lab uses methods suitable for Alaska soils. Cooperative Extension Publication FGV-00045, "Factors to Consider in Selecting a Soil Test Laboratory," provides advice on private labs, including the tests to request and the names of several labs that currently do Alaska soil testing. The private labs don't analyze the results or make recommendations for amendments. You'll need to send their test results to your local CES agent for that step.

Regardless of your lab choice, CES also offers a publication on soil sampling (FGV-00044) that provides a simple, step-by-step procedure for taking quality soil samples. You will find additional discussion of soil and how to prepare and amend it in Chapter 14, "Preparing Your Soil."

The moisture needs of plants are often described with phrases like *drought tolerant*; *requires moist, well-drained soil*; or *requires moist soil*. While these phrases are fairly self-explanatory, I'd like to note here that even drought-tolerant plants require moisture until they are well established, so be sure to water them well the first year or two.

Once you understand the parameters of your environment, focus on plants that prefer what you have. To get you started, the descriptions of some of my favorite plants and why I value them in Section 3 of this book include a quick reference showing each plant's horticultural needs. Of course, you'll want to expand your plant choices well beyond what's suggested in this book. A bit of research will help guide you. You can glean a lot of information about different plants from their labels, from the Internet, and from reference books.

Another way to learn more about the plants that thrive in your area is to visit your local nurseries and take the time to dally. Try to get to know the owner and the folks who work there. Tell them about your project and plans. They'll be happy to share their knowledge with you. I'm a big fan of local nurseries rather than the garden centers at big-box stores for a couple of reasons. Local nurseries have a much better grasp of what will do well in their area of Alaska. Most of the owners were gardeners first before they decided to turn a hobby into a commercial enterprise. They've probably grown a lot of their offerings. Though there are exceptions, in too many cases, the inventory at the national chain stores is ordered by someone in the state of Washington or even farther away. They don't know our growing conditions, at least not as well as a local gardener does. Yes, their prices may be attractive, but that may ultimately be an expensive bargain. We have many quality nurseries throughout the state that offer a broad array of hardy plants. Local retailers are always my first choice.

As you browse in the nursery, read the plant labels to discover important information about the plants that attract you. There is an Alaska exception to what you'll read and it has to do with light. Because of our northern latitude, commensurately angled sun, and generally cool summers, we can often grow plants in more hours of sunlight than the same plants will tolerate in other climates. A notable example is hosta, known south of here as a shade plant. In the Far North it can be grown in full sun. For the most part, however, following plant label guidelines is the best place to start. Make notes in your garden journal of candidate plant names (remember, botanical names are best to avoid ambiguity) so you can investigate them further.

At the beginning of this chapter, I mentioned using well-behaved plants. These are plants that stay where you plant them. They grow larger in place, rather than spreading wildly via marauding roots or by promiscuously producing thousands of babies. (Well, it *seems* like thousands!) Rambunctious plants that spread by runners, underground rhizomes, or root suckers can be a nightmare to manage or eradicate. Plants that have these thuggish characteristics are often the very ones people offer to share freely. The gift-giver has too many of them, so she passes them around. Beware of these "free" management headaches, as they make garden maintenance much more difficult.

Unfortunately, *well behaved* isn't one of the phrases you'll find on plant labels. If you read with care, though, you will see subtle warnings about the thugs. Phrases like *fills in quickly*, *naturalizes*, or *very vigorous* are often euphemisms for *rapid spreader*. So if you see this on a label, inquire further about the habits of the plant to see if you want it and what may well be its inherently difficult nature in your garden. There may be circumstances when you intentionally choose a plant with these characteristics, but it's important not to be surprised. To create a low-maintenance garden, focus on the many, many plants that add beauty without extra work.

If your local nursery has display gardens, stroll through them, observing and making note of what blooms when. Bloom time is one of the most difficult things to extract from reading as it's totally different for our gardens than books and articles written from an Outside point of view would indicate. They'll tell you daffodils will bloom in February. Not in Alaska! If you visit your nursery regularly, you'll get a much more accurate notion of when different plants will bloom in your area.

If you have the opportunity, visit local gardens. Learn what your gardening neighbors are growing successfully. Ask about and avoid plants that have been overly aggressive for them. Put Alaska's botanical gardens at the top of your list. They can provide you with a treasure trove of valuable information as well as plants. There's an

*Alaska's Botanical Gardens and Some of the Education-Oriented Public Gardens*

Anchorage: Alaska Botanical Garden

Fairbanks: The Georgeson Botanical Garden

Homer: The Pratt Museum Garden

Juneau: Glacier Gardens Rainforest Adventures

North of Juneau: Jensen-Olson Arboretum

Palmer: The Palmer Gardens

Skagway: Jewell Gardens

exceptional botanical garden in Anchorage called the Alaska Botanical Garden. The Georgeson Botanical Garden on the University of Alaska Fairbanks campus is also excellent and offers well-researched information on plants for the Interior and the Far North. Juneau also boasts a botanical garden, the fifty-acre Glacier Gardens Rainforest Adventures, situated in a lush rain forest.

Among the noteworthy public gardens in Alaska are several that also have an educational focus. Jewell Gardens in Skagway has colorful and traditional Alaska gardens absolutely billowing with perennials. Jensen-Olson Arboretum enjoys a lovely, picturesque seaside location about twenty-three miles north of Juneau. It's well worth the drive. The Palmer Garden is located on the grounds of The Palmer Museum of History and Art. It presents a fine collection of hardy perennials and grasses. The special little garden at the Pratt Museum in downtown Homer displays a collection of plants native to the Kenai Peninsula. Additional information about all of these public gardens can be found on the Internet. The Georgeson Botanical Garden website (www.georgesonbg.org) provides a convenient link to those mentioned here.

Join a local garden club and learn from the expert speakers they sponsor at their meetings. Go on the garden tours your club offers. Talk with other folks on the tours and ask questions. Most garden clubs are filled with people who have a passion for gardening and who are happy to share their knowledge with newer gardeners. If you're like me, you'll find taking notes will really help. I always think I'll remember a new plant and its name, but I find my notes are much more dependable. As you gather information, you will learn which plants you want to include in your garden beds and which ones you ought to avoid.

Another thing you might find helpful while visiting gardens is taking photos of plants you find appealing. Take overview images as well as close-ups of your favorite vignettes and combinations. Later, when you're back home thinking about the plans for your new garden, you can examine these images at your leisure. Try analyzing each one to see if you can determine what it is about the garden or part of a garden that's so attractive to you. Deconstructing the image into its individual parts is an exceptionally good way to pinpoint what you like and why. You can do the same thing with pictures in magazines and books. Fortified with the knowledge you've garnered from reading and visiting nurseries and gardens, along with the notes and photos you've assembled, you'll be more than ready to create detailed plans for each of your garden beds.

Deep-purple pansies cavort gaily with nasturtiums in shades of yellow and orange.

Once you have the location of your garden's main elements arranged and drawn onto your master plan, it's time to work out the details. In this phase you'll design each garden bed by making your plant selections and then drawing them onto the plan. Once again, give yourself the freedom to try different options and combinations until you're happy with your result.

For many gardeners this design phase is the best part of creating a new garden bed. You have a totally blank canvas on which to define what will become three-dimensional, ever-changing artistry. You have the freedom to go in any direction you wish as you dream and brainstorm. This is an opportunity to imagine an entire garden in your mind—one that has no weeds, I might add. But sometimes it seems like there are just too many choices.

So how do you crystallize what you want to create? When I'm working with clients, I ask them about their favorite and least favorite colors and plants. We discuss the importance of foliage, texture, fragrance, form, focal points, bloom time, and garden art. We also look at photos they may have torn from magazines—a great source of inspiration, by the way, if not for the specific plants, at least for a look or style. With these things in mind we make a list of plants that are well suited to the site. Then we build combinations of plants with contrasting and similar attributes. We place these groupings into the garden bed, repeating some periodically to add continuity to the design. Finally, we add other plants that will enhance the overall impact of the look we are working to create. In the next four chapters I'll explain the things to consider as you go through this process so you'll be ready to start adding details to your plan.

If you currently have a garden that you wish to enhance or change, most of the concepts for a new garden still apply to your situation. The difference is that you must decide which of your existing plants you will keep and which you want to eliminate. The "keepers" become part of the list of plants you'll work with as you develop your combinations and lay out your design. As you try different concepts and pairings, give yourself the freedom to consider moving the existing plants around. With the exception of mature trees and shrubs, most plants are pretty tolerant of transplanting. Hydrate them well beforehand and transplant on a cool, preferable slightly rainy day. Some gardens can be greatly enhanced with just a few well-selected additions. Others may need major editing, digging, and moving.

Some designers have strong opinions about what to use as the starting point for a garden bed design. My view is that all are equally valid, so start with what's most comfortable for you or for which you have the strongest feelings. If it's color, great. If

Two ceramic pots overflowing with annuals make an attractive space filler until the variegated dogwood (*Cornus alba* 'Bailhalo') in the foreground matures.

you've fallen in love with two or three specific plants, use them as your launch pad. If you like the look of a cottage garden, start with that premise. Go with what *you* like, be it color, style, or plants, and let the rest of the gardeners of the world do what they prefer in their gardens. I agree with the late Katharine Hepburn, who once said, "If you obey all the rules, you miss all the fun." So do it your way and have fun.

My primary caution is a horticultural one. Stick with plants that will thrive in your locale and your site's conditions. Some of your favorites from another part of the world may have to be traded in for something that looks similar and is hardy enough for your area of Alaska. On the other hand, you may find some great plants that thrive here but didn't do well in other places you might have gardened previously. Put the plants you select into an environment that will make them happiest. It should be one with the right amount of light and moisture. The plants also need to be well matched to your soil. (See Chapter 6, "Selecting Successful Plants," for further discussion of this topic.) Beyond those cautions, let your imagination and sense of style be your guide.

Your plant selections may include trees, shrubs, vines, perennial flowers, grasses, ferns, annuals, biennials, and/or bulbs. Some definitions and applications for each of these are in order.

An annual is a plant that in its native habitat completes its entire life cycle in one year. Not all annuals will make it through their full cycle during our short season; however, given enough time and heat, annuals started from seed will mature, bloom, and then set seed in order to propagate in the course of one season. The plant's purpose is to procreate. Because of this, you can keep an annual blooming all summer by removing the spent flowers, or deadheading it. In an effort to create seed the annual will continue to produce new blooms. Some well-known examples are pansies, marigolds, and nasturtiums.

Annuals are fun and provide long-lasting color. They are great in containers and along the front edge of a garden bed. You can also use annuals to fill areas around newly planted shrubs and perennials until they have reached maturity. Because annuals last only one season, they give you an opportunity to experiment with different color combinations without making a major investment. Their disadvantage is that they must be replaced each year.

A biennial lives two years, usually flowering in its second year. After it flowers and sets seed, it dies. To keep biennials reappearing consistently in your garden, plant the same variety in the same location during two consecutive years and let the plants go to seed. Be sure to mark where they are, so you don't accidentally weed out the seedlings. One of my favorite biennials is wild parsnip (*Angelica gigas*), a stunning late bloomer with enormous presence in the garden.

Perennials are plants whose life cycle is longer than two growing seasons. They are divided into two groups—herbaceous perennials and woody ornamentals.

An herbaceous perennial dies back to the ground during winter and emerges from the ground in spring. This turns out to be an excellent survival strategy in harsh climates. The stems are green and soft, though they may be rigid. Ferns, most grasses, many bulbs, and traditional hardy garden plants like iris, peonies, trollius, and delphiniums are all herbaceous perennials.

Some herbaceous perennials will bloom the first year from seed; most will not bloom for two, three, or even more years. Perennials will come back repeatedly without replacement if they are planted in an environment that meets their cultural needs. Remember that perennial does not mean eternal. Some are known as "short-lived," lasting only three or four years. Others that have a substantial life expectancy of forty years or more can succumb to disease or decline early if their cultural needs are not met. Many herbaceous perennials require periodic dividing and other maintenance

At seven feet-plus wild parsnip (*Angelica gigas*) produces a dramatic statement at the end of the season. (Photo courtesy of Christine Wickham.)

Rich golden-yellow trollius (*Trollius europaeus*) is an Alaska garden mainstay. They are easy to grow and are available in a range of shades, sizes, and bloom times.

to continue to thrive. A few will bloom for several months of the season, though most present their flowers for a shorter period—three to four weeks is fairly typical in our mild summers. Almost as if to make up for their shorter bloom periods they offer a rich variety of foliage, texture, bloom type and color, size, and shape. Some hug the ground while others have a bold silhouette, making them architecturally interesting in a garden tableau. And since they return year after year, growing lusher and fuller with the passage of time, herbaceous perennial plants are often used as the mainstay of a cold-climate garden.

Woody ornamentals have hard, woody stems that are usually covered with bark. These stems remain standing aboveground during the active growing season and during dormancy. Trees, shrubs, and many vines are woody ornamental perennials. Those that lose their leaves are called *deciduous*; those that don't are referred to as *evergreen*. Birch, alder, and clematis are deciduous. Most conifers, like spruce and

Trees add structure, a strong vertical element, and wonderful fall color.

Grasses add motion, fine texture, verticality, and lovely inflorescences throughout the growing season and into fall. Some grasses, like this feather reed grass (*Calamagrostis x acutiflora* 'Karl Foerster'), will stand tall through winter's snow.

pine, are evergreen, though an exception to this is the hardy larch tree, which turns vivid yellow in fall and then loses its needles.

Even though they must be protected from moose and snowshoe hares, trees and shrubs are important to consider when creating your design. These plants, sometimes referred to as woody perennials, have more mass than most other garden plants. Because of this their structure and placement can play a major role in establishing the framework for a garden. The arrangement of woody perennials is sometimes referred to as the "bones" of a garden. Trees and larger shrubs add a strong vertical element to a landscape, which in turn makes the overall design more dynamic. Two well-known groups of woody ornamentals, roses and lilacs, have beautiful, often fragrant blossoms. Though perhaps not as showy as roses and lilacs, most trees and shrubs produce flowers too. Berries, colorful foliage, and stems are among the many desirable attributes of trees and shrubs. Conifers add a special texture with their fine needles; they also provide color and structure in the garden in winter.

Another category of plants that can lend a vertical dimension to your garden is that of vines. Vines can be annual or perennial, herbaceous or woody. But they need not

always be trellised. You can let them scramble along the ground or through shrubs and other plants. The element of surprise when they bloom in unexpected places will add a note of whimsy to your plantings. The queen of the hardy vines, clematis, is available in many colors and differing bloom times.

Ornamental grasses have recently achieved widespread use in mixed gardens, and I urge you to try some of these easy-care plants. Like vines, they can be annual or perennial. Their slender, flexible foliage moves gracefully in even the gentlest breeze, contributing motion and, consequently, visual interest to a garden. The foliage of grass is often quite striking and is available in a range of colors, such as green, buff, rust, chocolate, gold, white, mauve, and variegated. On the other hand, their flowers, known as inflorescences, tend to be understated and often delicate looking. Carex, rushes, sedges, and cattails, though not true grasses, are often grouped with them for convenience.

Grasses are either clumping or running. The former are well behaved; the latter are not. Grasses are also categorized as either cool season or warm season. This has to do with the temperatures at which they do most of their growing, *not* their hardiness zone. Warm-season grasses do little below seventy degrees Fahrenheit and collapse when the weather turns cold in fall. Cool-season grasses begin to grow as soon as the snow melts and, unless broken down by heavy wet snow, will often stand throughout the winter. Cool-season grasses are definitely the better choice for coastal Alaska; warm-season grasses will do well inland, where temperatures are warmer during the growing season. Unfortunately, you may have to do some research to learn which is which as this is an attribute rarely noted on the plant tag.

Ferns are primitive plants that reproduce through spores rather than flowers and seeds. Their foliage, known as fronds, is elegant and lush, providing nice textural contrasts in the garden. When used as a background for a plant with delicate flowers, ferns really showcase and emphasize the flower blossoms. Though very acclimated to shade and moist areas, ferns can also be seen growing wild in Alaska's meadows in full sun. Most fronds are shades of green, but a few varieties offer silver overtones or shades of red or yellow.

Another group of plants to consider for your garden is bulbs. The word *bulb* is often misused to describe all kinds of fleshy underground structures including corms, tubers, rhizomes, and fleshy roots. While these structures vary, they do share a common trait with true bulbs: all store the substantial carbohydrates necessary to produce early and rapid growth in spring. This early growth makes this group of plants, especially classic spring bulbs like tulips and daffodils, a useful tool in northern garden design.

Because our growing season is short, anything we can do to extend the season will bring that much more pleasure. Our soils are particularly cold in spring and take a long time to warm. Perennials are slow getting started and annuals will just sit there,

Iris is an herbaceous perennial with a fleshy rhizome structure.

Lilies are true bulbs and are often sold potted up and sprouting.

Grape hyacinth (*Muscari armeniacum*) and checkered lilies (*Fritillaria meleagris*) join soft and fuzzy lamb's ear (*Stachys byzantina* 'Helen von Stein') and pale-yellow primrose (*Primula juliae* 'Dorothy').

Sweet and delicate-looking glory of the snow (*Chionodoxa*) starts the season early.

What a welcome sight after a long winter! The crocuses (*Crocus*) are already blooming as the snow recedes. Puppy Barney keeps an alert eye on a moose on the far side of the meadow.

The happy faces of daffodils (*Narcissus*) brighten any spring garden.

refusing to comply with our time table or even freeze if we plant them out too soon. Hardy bulbs, on the other hand, do extraordinarily well in the cool and sometimes downright cold air and soil of springtime in the Far North. These bright and welcome early bloomers are easy and fun. Many of the tiniest bulbs (sometimes called minor bulbs, but in my opinion much too special for that designation) will appear first, often pushing up through the melting snow. Some very special ones are glory of the snow (*Chionodoxa*), Siberian squill (*Scilla sibirica*), grape hyacinth (*Muscari*), crocus (*Crocus*), and the checkered lily (*Fritillaria meleagris*), a close relative to our native chocolate lily but without its offensive fragrance.

Daffodils (*Narcissus*) are next out of the ground. If you select some early-, mid-, and late-season daffodils you can prolong the pleasure of their happy faces for weeks on end. Given excellent drainage, these will return year after year and multiply as well. Our friends the moose will leave them alone, but remember, tulips aren't so lucky. In fact, moose adore tulips! So, unless you have a well-fenced garden or are willing to share, you may want to forgo tulips.

Aside from extending the season, bulbs serve another purpose. They'll fill what may look like big gaps between your perennials in the early part of the season. In so doing, they may help you avoid a common urge to plant things too closely together

Clockwise:

Gay daffodils (*Narcissus*) and vibrant tulips (*Tulipa* 'Come Back') fill the bare spaces between emerging perennials in early spring in the author's garden.

Vibrant fall colors will add another dimension to your garden.

'Fireglow' cushion spurge (*Euphorbia griffithii* 'Fireglow') is stunning in its fall finery.

when you first put them into your garden bed. The incredible length of our early-summer days combined with late-season rains cause our gardens to transform from sparse, even meager, to packed magnificence in the span of three months. Using bulbs to satisfy your need for fuller, lush gardens in June will provide the added benefit of less chaos at Labor Day.

Another consideration for extending your season is to use foliage that turns brilliant shades in the fall. Autumn in Alaska is short, but it can be dazzling. Many trees and shrubs provide an added burst of brilliant color as the summer wanes, turning swiftly to fall and

Flowering trees perfume the air at Fritz Creek Gardens in springtime. (Photo courtesy of Rita Jo Shoultz.)

A grouping of containers filled with easy-care annuals can contribute season-long beauty to your home. For some busy Alaskans this may be an ideal way to have color with very little maintenance.

then to winter. Some herbaceous perennials have fabulous fall color as well. While our flush of autumn color is generally much briefer than in more southern latitudes, it is nonetheless quite enjoyable.

Garden beds and, in fact, the overall landscape can be designed using all the different groups of plants described in this chapter or just a few of them. Some gardeners use only annuals in containers on the deck or patio, as I did very early in my Alaska gardening days. Others concentrate on herbaceous perennials with just a few bulbs for springtime while refraining from woody plants because of the prevalence of moose on their land. On the other hand, many fenced gardens enjoy the strong structural presence of trees and shrubs. My preference is to take advantage of all the groups, mixing them together in order to benefit from the attributes each has to offer. Using all types of plants lets me create innumerable combinations that bring me pleasure from the moment the snow melts away until well after it returns in fall. But that is my choice; your tastes and circumstances may suggest a different, equally valid approach.

The season opens with a medley
of blues and lavender.

Most of us consider color a vital garden ingredient. In this part of the world, which is covered by snow for a majority of the year, it becomes even more important. Some designers focus more on texture, foliage, or the architecture of plants, letting color happen almost accidentally. Certainly, beautiful gardens can be created this way, and indeed foliage and plant structure are critical components in achieving stellar results. If you are like most people, however, and have strong likes and dislikes in colors, it is a good idea to consider color early in the game.

Color from the blossoms of a given plant can be ephemeral, staying with us a mere few weeks, while its foliage, shape, and structure are present throughout the season. Nonetheless, if you plan carefully for a succession of blooms you can carry a particular color scheme throughout the season. You can also change the color palette completely between spring and summer and yet again in fall.

As you think about color for your garden beds, ask yourself some questions. Do you want a vibrant, joyful place in which to entertain many friends or a quiet, restful retreat for your family's pleasure? Are you more traditional in your tastes or do you like to break all the rules? Do you have a favorite color or combination of colors? Do you prefer lots of different colors together or a limited palette? The answers to these questions will influence your choice of colors.

Different colors evoke different moods and emotions in each of us; we don't all respond in the same way to the same color, nor do we all have the same favorite color. That said, red is traditionally a color of passion and excitement while orange is vital and challenging. Green is safe and soothing.

Summer is brightened with white, yellow, and a touch of pink.

In fall burgundy and mauve enrich the yellow and pink of summer.

Vibrant orange and cheerful yellow can be combined to a pleasing effect when balanced with blue and purple.

A very romantic and soothing combination can be produced with rose and white.

Purple is regal while yellow is cheerful and gay. Pink, blue, and white are said to be quiet, cool, and romantic, respectively.

In a garden, however, colors don't stand alone. How they appear to us is deeply influenced by their neighbors and the light. For example, purple, my favorite color, is very regal and sophisticated when combined with blue. With red, purple becomes rich and sassy. With its color wheel complement, yellow, purple is electric. Juxtaposed to lavender and lilac, purple is soothing and restful. So you can use your favorite color to create compositions of varying moods.

Once again Alaska provides some special opportunities. Colors have a different quality here because our light is so different. The low angle of the sun is a major part of this. So is our clean air. Many of us live near the sea and enjoy the mists of maritime proximity as well. All of these conditions work collectively to make colors appear more saturated. Where soft pinks and pastels can look washed out and bland in the intense overhead sun of other parts of the world, here they are vibrant in sunlight and in shade they just sparkle. Picture the elegant queen of the prairie (*Filipendula rubra* 'Venusta') holding its frothy pink plumes seven feet in the air in full sun. Or imagine the impact of a pale pink astilbe (*Astilbe chinensis* 'Vision in Pink') glowing above rich, deep-green foliage in your shade garden.

Reds, purples, and oranges are rich and full-bodied at our latitudes. They don't take on the harsh, jangling feeling some may perceive elsewhere. The bright red of 'Jacob Cline' bee balm (*Monarda didyma* 'Jacob Cline') combined with deep purple 'Caradonna' salvia (*Salvia nemorosa* 'Caradonna') is downright opulent in our soft light. Here yellows and whites seem to leap out of the garden at you. As a result, for me yellow and white look better en masse or used sparingly rather than dotted around a garden. White fireweed (*Epilobium angustifolium* var. *album*) is an elegant and eye-catching plant. When planted in a large stand its airy, upright form and gleaming white color make an incredibly dramatic show in northern light.

Clockwise:

Queen of the prairie (*Filipendula rubra* 'Venusta') flaunts its frothy pink plumage high above the garden. Soft northern light accentuates this pale pastel.

Dramatic white fireweed (*Epilobium augustifolium* var. *album*) presents a lush screen at the back of a white-themed border.

Purple and red make a wonderfully rich and sassy combination.

The soft light of the Far North makes yellow splashes on the leaves of variegated Japanese coltsfoot (*Petasites japonicus* var. *giganteus* 'Variegata') sparkle in sunlight and in shade.

Backlighting causes flowers in a container to glow in the afternoon sun. (Photo courtesy of Beverly Ambrose.)

### My Favorite Books on Color

*Fearless Color Gardens* by Keeyla Meadows (Timber Press)

*Colors for the Garden* by P. Allen Smith (Clarkson Potter)

*Blueprints for Paradise* by Sara Steele (Tide-Mark Press, Ltd.)

*The Well-Designed Mixed Garden* by Tracy DiSabato-Aust (Timber Press)

The protracted dawns and sunsets we experience during the growing season offer many opportunities to use backlighting to change the nature of color in a different way. To create this special effect, position the plants in the garden so the sun passes behind them relative to the place from which you'll view the garden. That is, gardens to the east or west of you will light up as the sun rises or sets. Using backlighting you can make a burgundy shrub like barberry (*Berberis thunbergii* 'Crimson Velvet') glow red. The same manipulation for effect will cause orange or scarlet blooms to appear fiery. Tall, graceful ornamental grasses dazzle like fireworks when the sun shines through them. Highly textured plants look as if they have a halo when backlit. The effect will last for more than an hour, whereas Outside it can be quite fleeting. If you want to see how effective backlighting can be, position a potted plant between you and the low sun and watch it light up.

When considering color, take into account the color of your home. Your home is usually the largest single object in your landscape, and it will have a major impact on how things will appear arranged about it. An effective technique is to use the color of your home's trim in the plantings, garden art, or even structural elements. This firmly ties the gardens to the house. Fortunately, many homes are painted or stained in fairly neutral colors, giving the gardener a free hand in color choices for the garden.

Clockwise:

The buds of 'Arctic Glow' globe thistle (*Echinops spaerocephalus* 'Arctic Glow'), the seed pods of a tall mullein (*Verbascum*), and a spider's web all take on an otherworldly look when backlit by bright afternoon sun.

It might seem impossible to improve on the incredible color of Himalayan blue poppies (*Meconopsis longifolium*), but you can if you place them to take advantage of the backlighting potential of our low-angled sunlight.

The rusty-brown foliage on the trees repeats the trim color of the home while blue-green hosta matches the siding.

Chartreuse buds on 'Bicolor' monkshood (*Aconitum x cammarum* 'Bicolor') are emphasized by the neighboring golden-leaved hosta.

While flowers are an obvious source of color in your garden beds, foliage can also add variety and pizzazz to the color scheme. Besides the many different shades of green available, increasingly more plants offer foliage options in bronze, chocolate, rust, burgundy, chartreuse, pink, silver, gold, and more. Variegated combinations can make foliage an even more interesting component in your design. In fact, repeating the flower colors in your foliage selections will help to create a feeling of harmony in your garden bed. For example, as can be seen in the photo on the left, you can unite the blue and white flowers of 'Bicolor' monkshood (*Aconitum x cammarum* 'Bicolor') with the green and white 'Patriot' hosta (*Hosta* 'Patriot') foliage to emphasize the white in both the flowers and the edges of the hosta leaves. A more subtle combination with the same monkshood uses 'Gold Standard' hosta (*Hosta* 'Gold Standard') to make the chartreuse flower buds stand out.

Not only can you use foliage color to complement or repeat the colors in your blooms, you can contrast one foliage hue with another. For example, I find the strong contrast between chartreuse and burgundy ninebark (*Physocarpus opulifolius* 'Dart's Gold' and *Physocarpus opulifolius* 'Diablo') very appealing. The point is, if you utilize the palette of foliage color available to you *consciously*, it can add a dimension of richness to your garden that may otherwise elude you.

Foliage, even during the height of bloom, is an incredibly important element in creating a stunning garden, but when flowers are few, creative use of foliage is essential to keep the garden enticing. Leaves lend texture, dimension, shape, and structure to your tableau. Some are huge, like those of ornamental rhubarb (*Rheum palmatum* 'Atrosanguineum'), which in Alaska regularly exceed two feet in length and over one foot in width. Just one of these plants makes a real statement in a perennial or mixed border.

Conversely, leaves can also appear as fragile as gossamer, like the lovely Artemisia silvermound (*Artemisia schmidtiana*), but still be very hardy. There are the upright

The foliage of 'Diablo' (*Physocarpus opulifolius* 'Diablo') and 'Dart's Gold' ninebark (*Physocarpus opulifolius* 'Dart's Gold') produce a vibrant contrasting combination while chartreuse and gold are repeated to engender harmony in this composition.

Ornamental rhubarb (*Rheum palmatum* 'Atrosanguineum') foliage is big, bold, and colorful. It can be a great focal point.

Siberian bugloss (*Brunnera macrophylla* 'Jack Frost') mingles with Labrador violets (*Viola labradorica*).

swords of iris (*Iris*), the narrow arching leaves of daylilies (*Hemerocallis*), and the tiny leaflets of thyme (*Thymus*) and snow-in-summer (*Cerastium tomentosum*). Elephant's ears or Pigsqueak (*Bergenia*) have big, flat, paddle-shaped leaves that turn a deep red in fall. One beautiful combination places the silvery heart-shaped leaves of Siberian bugloss (*Brunnera macrophylla* 'Jack Frost') so it mingles with the smaller, deep-purple heart-shaped foliage of Labrador violet (*Viola labradorica*). In this combination, the same shape is repeated in differing sizes and colors.

Lady's mantle (*Alchemilla mollis*) has sweet scalloped leaves that hold the tiniest droplets of moisture on their surface. They have an exquisite fairyland quality when covered with morning dew or after a soft rain.

Stonecrops (*Sedum*) provide us with some wonderful thick, meaty-looking foliage as well as good color variety. Lambs' ears (*Stachys byzantina*) are so soft and fuzzy it's impossible not to touch them. Sea holly (*Eryngium*) and globe thistle (*Echinopsis*) sport unique spiny foliage. Many plants have elegant deeply serrated leaves that add still another dimension. Grasses, which will sway gracefully in the breeze, not only offer a different shape and texture but also add the element of movement to your scene.

The blending of blue-green spikes of blue oat grass (*Helictotrichon sempervirens*) and the soft and fuzzy silvery-blue of lambs' ears (*Stachys byzantina* 'Helen von Stein')

along with iridescent-blue sea holly (*Eryngium* 'Sapphire Blue') offers great textural variety with similar bluish hues.

The needles of conifers offer another avenue for adding more interest to a garden bed. Members of this group of largely evergreen trees and shrubs have a unique texture that is quite striking when mixed with herbaceous perennials. Many varieties of spruce (*Picea*) are on the "last to eat" list of our moose and so might be a good choice for those of you who can't reasonably protect your garden. There are some spectacular dwarf varieties in a broad range of colors, including blue, silver, gold, and various shades of green. An excellent and very hardy example is dwarf Colorado blue spruce (*Picea pungens glauca* 'Montgomery'), which grows naturally in a conical shape. At six feet tall and five feet wide at maturity, this variety is small enough to fit into most landscapes yet the impact of its finely textured, silvery-blue needles has real power in combination with broader-leaved plants.

Here is a wonderful interplay of color and texture in yellow and chocolate. (Photo courtesy of Christine Wickham.)

The challenge, then, is in taking all these options and melding them into a design that is pleasing to you. What is it that makes one grouping interesting and another not? The first is variety. A combination of plants with different textures, leaf sizes, and overall plant shape will be much more stimulating than one in which all the plants have similar foliage sizes and shapes. A friend of mine distills it to three words—spiky, frilly, and moundy. With these adjectives, she's describing the structure or appearance of each plant. Examples of "spiky" include upright grasses, delphinium (*Delphinium*), and iris (*Iris*). A frilly plant has lacy or deeply cut leaves with an airy feel, like columbine (*Aquilegia*) or masterwort (*Astrantia*). The "moundy" member of the trio has more substance and a rounded shape, like a hosta (*Hosta*) or coral bells (*Heuchera*). Make combinations of plants with these three characteristics and you are on your way to something captivating.

Adding a variety of textures, sizes, and shapes in the flower selections of a grouping will provide another layer of sophistication to your design. In the combination in the photo on this page look at the bold blooms of a 'Golden Tycoon' lily (*Lilium* L.A. Hybrid 'Golden Tycoon') next to the tiny blossoms of 'Fire Cracker' loosestrife (*Lysimachia ciliata* 'Purpurea'). Not only do the sizes of the flowers contrast, so do the shape and color of the foliage. In addition to variety the best combinations also include repetition of one or more of the elements. This note of similarity helps your eye connect one plant to the other. In this combination the distinctive chocolate-brown stamens of the lily echo the dark foliage of the loosestrife and 'Centerglow' ninebark (*Physocarpus opulifolius* 'Center Glow') as well as the stems of the tall flower spikes of ligularia (*Ligularia przewalskii*) in the background. Yellow is the other chord of commonality as it replays in the flowers of several of the plants and the grass at the far left of the image.

*Foliage* by Nancy J. Ondra (Story Publishing)

*Perennial Combinations* by C. Colston Burrell (Rodale Press, Inc.)

*Grasses* by Nancy J. Ondra (Storey Publishing)

To develop an eye for this mix of disparate and repeating themes, look analytically at photos in gardening magazines and books. Study planters, containers, and small garden areas that you find appealing. Try to understand what contrasts and combinations awaken a response in you. Also look carefully at examples that fall flat and analyze what is missing. It won't take long until this becomes second nature to you.

If you're feeling really adventuresome and want to have fun and stretch your comfort zone, try designing a garden bed with foliage as the first element under consideration. Make it compelling, through foliage, when *nothing* is in bloom. This goes a long way toward solving the issue of bloom times since the garden will be interesting without flowers. If this does not seem intuitively obvious, think about a black-and-white photograph. Isn't it the shapes, textures, and light contrasts that make a black-and-white photo so arresting? Try to apply this concept to your foliage combinations.

Another word about black-and-white photography: it can be employed remedially. If you are dissatisfied with one of your garden beds, make a black-and-white image of it. (Most easy-to-use photo management programs will allow you to render a color digital image in black and white.) You will certainly see it in a different light—literally—and totally different elements of the composition will make themselves obvious to you. Do you have enough variety in your foliage? More important, is it compelling? Have you used combinations that excite you? Think about foliage as you select plants for your garden beds. It is one of the most critical elements in creating a show-stopping design.

Woody plants add structure and
fullness to this small garden bed.

# 10

Of course, plants are not all flowers and leaves. Stems, bark, seed heads, and berries can add color, structure, texture, or form to your designs. Because of our ever-present moose, many Alaska gardens have far fewer shrubs and trees than you might find in a similarly sized garden that's not in moose country. But if you are able to protect them, these plants can add enormously to the impact of your landscape.

Some woody plants, including Alaska natives, have colorful or highly textured bark that you can feature in your color schemes. Our beautiful paper birch (*Betula papyrifera*) with its white peeling outer covering is unique and highly prized Outside. It's a tree I think we should use more, especially in larger gardens. Quaking aspen (*Populus tremuloides*), known for its delightful quivering leaves, has attractive smooth greenish trunks and limbs. Amur cherry (*Prunus maackii*) has distinctive deep golden bark with slightly raised horizontal markings. It's quite beguiling. Planting a large clump of perennials nearby whose flowers have hues similar to the stems of a woody plant will draw your eye to the combination, thus increasing the impact of both elements.

The flower color of this Asiatic lily (*Lilium asiatic* 'Corida') highlights the nearby bronze trunks of Amur cherry (*Prunus mackii*) to increase the impact of both.

Luminous white bark is accented with dark peelings on one of our beautiful paper birch (*Betula papyrifera*) trees.

The rich color of textured alder bark is repeated in deep purple baneberry (*Actaea simplex* 'Hillside Black Beauty').

Alder, a ubiquitous native shrub, is rarely considered as a landscape plant, but despite its suckering habits it has interesting possibilities in some situations. Its sable bark is subtly textured and its dark-green, coarsely toothed foliage is very good-looking. As a bonus, alder tolerates moose browsing! I mentioned earlier that you can site a garden in order to use an existing clump of alder as a backdrop, but you can also prune it to look more tree-like. If you then plant some perennials close to the base of the pruned alder, it will visually become an integral part of the combination.

Trees and shrubs often sport conspicuous seed pods such as berries after their flowers fade. This provides another opportunity for you to experiment with color combinations, texture, and shape. While some plants bear fruit in midsummer, much of the action is reserved for fall.

Like other plant elements, berries are available in a variety of colors, including white, green, blue, orange, pink, purple, red, and more. The brilliant scarlet berry clusters of the beautiful showy mountain ash (*Sorbus decora*) are dazzling bathed in the warm rays of a late-summer sun. If you are a bird lover, you'll also delight in the flocks of birds that these and other fruit-bearing trees and shrubs will attract in late fall and early winter when alternative food sources are sparse. Differently shaped seed pods, though rarely as colorful as berries, appear in a vast assortment of forms. There are spike-covered orbs, long fuzzy drupes, and winged configurations that flutter in the gentlest breeze.

In addition to visual delights, gardens can provide pleasure through our olfactory sense. It is said that fragrance evokes some of our most powerful memories. As I can readily conjure up the smell of my mother's delicious tomatoes, perhaps you remember the soft perfume of a lilac in your grandmother's garden or the delightful fresh scent of an old friend's peony. Including a "memory" plant in your garden beds can carry you off to lovely recollections. Perhaps more important, including fragrant plants in your garden can create future memories for your children and grandchildren. What could be a nicer heritage?

There are many aromatic flowering plants that are hardy in Alaska. In addition to lilacs and peonies, many lilies, violas, and primroses are intensely sweet smelling. Dianthus, bleeding hearts, phlox, roses, and even hosta add their perfume to the garden. Mock orange shrubs (*Philadelphus lewisii* 'Blizzard') have such a glorious scent when they are in full bloom that a gardener I know has a spontaneous party each season to celebrate the event in her garden. The vigorous and stunning sulfur-yellow Tibetan primrose (*Primula florindae*) is intoxicating when it blooms, and it does so for a long time. I enjoy having a large planting of them next to my pond near where I like to sit early on summer mornings with a cup of tea. I can't think of a better way to start the day than with the soothing music of a waterfall and the heady perfume of a favorite flower.

Foliage can also add a note of fragrance. Herbs release a rush of aroma if you crush their leaves between your fingers. Some will exude a lovely sachet if you simply brush them as you walk by. Lavender is one of these. It's marginally hardy in much of Alaska, not at all in the Interior, and requires sharp drainage, but I enjoy its bouquet so much I add some to the garden each year and accept that it might not make it through winter. And how very satisfying and self-indulgent it is to soak in a hot bath infused with the essence of lavender at the end of the gardening day.

Bright berries will attract birds to your garden in fall and winter. These elderberries (*Sambucus racemosa*) are a favorite treat of waxwings and many other birds.

Lovely and delightfully fragrant English lavender (*Lavandula angustifolia* 'Hidcote Superior') is marginally hardy in most parts of Alaska. Situating it with excellent drainage will improve success.

A cardoon, chard, thyme, Italian parsley, nasturtiums, and columbine thrive in a compact four-by-four-foot raised bed. Mixing food crops with ornamentals can achieve wonderful foliage medleys.

Herbs. What a funny name for one of nature's treasures. It doesn't seem like we even say it right, does it? Shouldn't it be pronounced like the man's name with an *h*? Well, even though we leave the *h* out of our pronunciation, don't leave herbs out when you plan your garden. You may say, "But I don't cook!" It doesn't matter.

The reasons to include herbs are myriad and I'm not sure in which order to list them because order can denote priority. In this case, I think all the reasons are equally important. So here goes. Herbs are pretty. They have interesting foliage and varied flowers. They attract beneficial insects. They smell great. You can use them to cook, fresh or dried. Herbs have lots of medicinal qualities. You can brew teas with them— for you, not the garden. You can add them to a fragrant potpourri or to your bathwater. And they dry well for winter use in cooking or flower arrangements. Besides, most are quite easy to grow from seed and they don't take much room. So why not grow herbs?

I started growing these flavorful plants because my husband is a fabulous cook and often when he needed a fresh herb for a dish he had in mind, it was not available at our grocery store, living as we do at the literal end of the road. There is nothing to compare to his pasta with tomatoes and *fresh* basil as anyone who has had it will attest. Because I love this dish, I grow lots and lots of basil in the greenhouse, enough to make pesto sauce too. Pesto freezes well, giving us the opportunity to experience that glorious, pungent flavor in winter. What a treat! Herbs also make great hostess gifts. Your hostess may appreciate a nice bottle of wine when you arrive at her home for dinner, but wait until you experience the response when you take a big, thriving basil plant or a pot of mixed herbs!

If you are not yet convinced to grow these versatile plants, let me add that they tolerate transplanting and do quite well in containers. This comes in handy at the end of the season. You can dig up a few of each kind that you use for cooking, put them into a pot, and invite them indoors for the winter. Oftentimes they will stay viable until spring, though a few gasp a bit during our very limited December sunlight. Be sure to inspect each plant *very* carefully for harmful insects and remove them before bringing the plant indoors, where the insects will definitely flourish.

I mentioned vegetables earlier in the context of locating a vegetable garden in a sunny, protected, and relatively flat area, but there's another option, at least for some of your food crops. Though usually grown in northern gardens as annuals, many vegetables are quite attractive and can be novel additions to a sunny mixed ornamental bed. The stiff spiny leaves and thistle-like fruit of cardoons and artichokes have

Kale, chard, and lettuce are all bold-leafed, delightfully textured candidates for the perennial garden. They will stay presentable for a long time if you harvest the leaves from the outside lower foliage.

Deep-orange annuals brighten a bed of broccoli.

fabulous architectural presence. The leafy vegetables—spinach, chard, and lettuce as well as Chinese greens—come in a broad array of colors, have ample-sized foliage, and can be tucked in easily. Kale, with its bold leathery character, is a particularly engaging plant.

Vegetables that mature early in the season can be paired with later-developing perennials, which will fill in any holes left by harvesting. Food crops normally gathered in fall can contribute their beauty for the entire growing season. Use caution, though, when planting root crops like carrots and beets in a perennial bed. Locate them where they have plenty of space since the harvesting process may disturb the roots of nearby perennials.

If you are uncomfortable with the notion of putting vegetables into your flower beds, consider the reverse idea. Sprinkle some brightly colored annuals throughout your vegetable garden to transform it from purely functional to radiantly festive. You can produce very exciting results. Whether planting herbs or vegetables in your ornamental garden beds or adding annuals to the vegetable patch, be adventurous and try something different each year.

A dramatic foliage combination created with deep-green, spikey leek foliage, pretty round nasturtium leaves, and scalloped tomato greens make this greenhouse a feast for the eyes as well as the table. Brilliant scarlet fruit and blossoms amp up the overall effect.

Some flowers, like self-sowing pansies, violas, and the nasturtiums and calendulas in this artichoke bed, are also edible. They make tasty and colorful additions to salads and other dishes.

Be sure to make room for garden art and personal mementos in your plan as they will personalize your garden.

At this point in your gardening plan, you've made decisions about what colors you'd like in your garden and you've thought about foliage, bark, berries, and fragrance as well as what role each will play. You have in mind the techniques you plan to employ to unify your garden. By now you've decided on the look you want to achieve and have thought about scale. You should have a list of plants you might want to use. You've learned enough about these selections to determine they will be successful in your garden because their horticultural needs will be met by your environment. You've made notes of how big (width and height) each plant will become and when it should bloom. It's now time to finish putting these details on paper. Get out your master plan and affix a sheet of tracing paper over it. Smooth the tracing paper so you can clearly see your master plan through it. Grab your favorite pencil and a big eraser. Ready? Let's do it!

If you're going to incorporate trees or shrubs, I suggest you place them on the plan first, as they will help define the structure of your garden. Give their placement a lot of consideration so they have plenty of room to grow. When adding shrubs and trees to your landscape it is critical to know how big they will become. Always read the plant label to see what it says about their anticipated size. For trees, the usual label practice is to provide the size expected at ten years of age. Because our growing season is so short, it may take your woody plants longer than ten years to achieve their mature size, but unless the moose "prune" them, they will eventually get there. I also recommend double-checking the label data with information you can find on the Internet as well as in reference books about trees and shrubs. A superb reference for this subject is *Dirr's Hardy Trees and Shrubs: An Illustrated Encyclopedia* by Michael A. Dirr. Do pay attention to and act on what you've learned. There is nothing sadder than a mature tree that is too big for its location.

So, if the information about a particular tree indicates it will grow to twenty-five feet in width, draw a circle to scale that is at least twenty-five feet in diameter. If you plan to include perennials or annuals you may choose to plant some of these under the tree. In that case you will draw the circles for those plants within the tree's circle. Also take note of the eventual height of the tree and be sure it won't block any of the views you want to preserve. Next, do the same thing with each shrub you will use. Determine where you want them and make scale circles for each on the tracing paper. Remember, it's okay to try different approaches until you're satisfied with the result. Tracing paper comes in rolls and is very inexpensive, so go ahead and discard or erase false starts. A very excellent, internationally known designer whom I admire admits

**For More About
Woody Plants**

*Dirr's Hardy Trees and Shrubs: An
Illustrated Encyclopedia* by Michael A.
Dirr (Timber Press)

*Complete Guide to Trees and Shrubs*
(Meredith Books)

*Landscape Plants for Alaska: A List of
Trees, Shrubs, Vines, and Groundcovers
for Alaskan Landscapes,* Publication
#HGA-00035 by the University of Alaska
Fairbanks Cooperative Extension Service

to using an *electric* eraser! We all have to fiddle with the design to achieve the look and feel we want, so give yourself the freedom to do the same. Once you are happy with the location of the woody plants, write their names in the circles. Now draw in any garden art you plan to use as well as featured rocks, benches, and other elements of your new hardscape.

Then add another layer of tracing paper before you start drawing the perennials into the garden beds. I suggest using layers of tracing paper so you can restart a particular phase of the design without having to redraw all the parts you have already perfected. If you drew your master plan in a scale that is smaller than one-quarter inch to one foot (one-quarter inch to five feet, for example), you may find it helpful to make a separate base drawing in a larger scale of those areas that need a lot of detail. For individual garden beds a scale of one-quarter inch to one foot works well for me. With a little experimenting you will find a scale that suits your needs.

Because of the difficulties in keeping moose away from woody plants, many gardeners within their habitat utilize more herbaceous perennials than trees and shrubs. Your garden may have a lot of herbaceous perennials as well. With so many options and other things to think about it can sometimes be a bit overwhelming to figure out how to incorporate everything you want. I find breaking the process down into smaller increments works well.

To do this I start with a favorite plant or one I want to highlight. Then I select two or four other plants that will make an interesting combination with it. (Remember the discussion on spiky, frilly, and moundy in Chapter 9, "Fabulous Foliage"?) If I really like the combination I may use it exactly as-is several times throughout the garden or repeat it with a variation. The variation might be to replace one of the plants with an alternate or use the same kind of plants, changing only the color of one of them. Either way the repetition will help establish unity. Repeating a combination is especially effective when planning a long border because the duplication of a familiar pattern draws your eye along the length of the garden bed. Also, let me add that if you're designing a large garden bed, using more than one of each plant in

Bulbs can enhance a spring scene even in a mature garden.

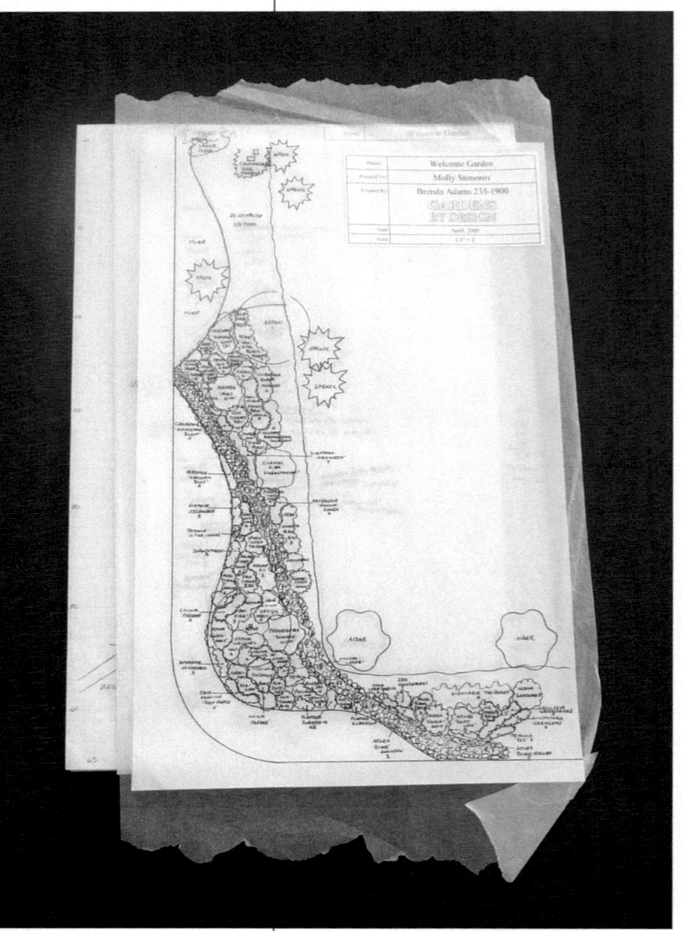

Make a final drawing of your plan, incorporating all the layers onto a single sheet. It can be fun to add some artistic flourishes to the drawing. Be sure to make several photocopies of your plan for future reference and to have one to use during planting.

the combination will give you much more impact. You might use three, five, or more of each depending on the size of your project.

Now draw your combinations onto the plan, again making scale circles to represent each plant at its mature size. When you are satisfied with their placement write in the plant names or a number keyed to the list of plants you plan to use. Repeat this process with different combinations, supplementing with other individual plants as well until the beds are complete.

If you want a garden that will be lush and full, your circles should touch each other or even overlap a little bit. If your style dictates spaces between your plants or combinations, then draw them with the desired spaces on the plan. By using this scale drawing approach, and following the plan when you plant, your garden will grow into the vision you have of it without your having to keep moving plants that have outgrown their spaces.

New gardens as well as spring gardens can seem terribly sparse. To fill in bare spaces, create more lushness, and add color in a new garden, annuals can serve as an inexpensive yet attractive device to employ until your perennials and woody plants mature. They also offer the freedom to create different color combinations each year until the garden gets fully established.

That said, a mature garden calls for a different technique to make it look more interesting in the spring. That's right—bulbs!

It's best to design bulbs into your plan from the beginning even though they won't be planted until the fall. Whether you plan on bulbs from the start or decide to add them later, locate them in the bed so their fading foliage will be camouflaged by a late-emerging perennial. This is especially important with bulbs that have large leaves like those of daffodils, so you won't be tempted to cut the fading foliage back before it's had the time necessary to replenish the bulb for next year's show. After the foliage has yellowed, it has completed its task and can be removed.

Once you finish constructing your plan on tracing paper, you may wish to check your color combinations by using colored pencils or even crayons to fill in the plant circles. The colors won't be exact, but this step will help you see if one color is too dominant or not well distributed in your design. Make adjustments and changes as necessary.

Next, count the quantities of each plant you will use and add this information to your plant list. This will be extremely helpful when you go to the nursery to do your plant shopping.

At this point you can make a final drawing of your master plan with all its details incorporating all of the layers into one document. I use vellum, a substantial but translucent type of paper, so I can trace my work. As you redraw your design feel free to use some of your artistic talent, employing different symbols for plants with varying forms and textures. For example, you might draw pointy edges on a circle that represents a grass or an iris or add scalloped edges for a plant with big, bold leaves. There's certainly no need to do this, but you might find it enjoyable.

When you are finished drawing, make multiple photocopies of the final plan for future reference and for use during planting. I find both the plan and plant list to be useful tools over time as the garden develops and matures.

# Building and Managing a Low-Maintenance Northern Garden

Visitors are welcomed to this charming Alaska log home by a colorful and low-maintenance garden. The informal style of the garden is perfectly suited to the architecture of the house.

Once you have completed your design and have the results of your soil tests, you are ready to dig in. If you haven't done so already, take some "before" photos of the area you plan to landscape. A few years from now you'll be amazed when you look back and see the difference. It's also fun to have images of the project as it progresses. And when you've completed your enterprise, be sure to document your newly created garden as well.

The first step is to lay out your plan on the ground. There are a variety of ways to do this. Some people like to use garden hoses to define the garden beds and pathways; this works fine if you have enough hoses and it's warm enough for them to be pliable. An alternative that I find more flexible is to paint the design onto the ground using inverted marking paint. (In case you're unfamiliar with this, it's canned spray paint designed to be used in the upside-down position.) In either case, using your completed master plan, measure where the main elements should go and draw them with hose or paint. When using paint, it helps to have two colors, one for the first pass and the second for corrections or adjustments to the plan. I also recommend wearing old shoes and walking on the upwind side of the can as you paint! Next, put five-gallon buckets, big trash cans, or similar objects in the locations you've planned for trees, shrubs, or other major features. Now look at the layout from inside your home, from the approach to your house, the deck, or any other location from which you'll often see your garden to be sure it achieves your goals. Carefully check the view corridors to make certain they're clear. Determine if everything feels in balance. This is the time to make any changes. Hopefully, there won't be many, but there are usually a few things that weren't obvious when you put your plan on paper.

Depending on the scope of your undertaking and your comfort with construction, you may want to hire a contractor for some of the structural components. Building fences, decks, patios, retaining walls, or ponds, laying stone, moving big rocks, or terracing a hillside are often beyond the scope of the do-it-yourself gardener. If you hire a contractor, try to find one who specializes in landscape work so he or she is sensitive to the issues associated with this kind of activity. Some of the contractors who specialize in landscaping are quite artistic and can be a real asset to your overall project. Either way, it's best to have these structural elements completed early in the process and certainly before you begin planting.

As mentioned earlier, be sure to think through the order in which the different elements need to be constructed, especially if this will be a multiyear project. Access for needed equipment is vital.

A good match between the
quality and fertility of your soil
and the needs of your plants will
encourage vigorous growth and
healthy plants.

Among the most important elements for successful gardening are the nature and quality of the garden's soil. Soil is the medium through which plants receive their sustenance. In order for plants to absorb the nutrients they need, those nutrients must be present and available in the soil. If a plant's needs are not met, the plant will be more susceptible to disease and insect damage and may ultimately die. Conversely, a good soil-plant match will encourage vigorous growth and good health in your plants.

Alaska soils vary dramatically even on a small property. They range from sandy gravel to dense clay, from well drained to water saturated. What can be said generally is that our topsoil layer is relatively thin due to recent glaciation and it is also somewhat acidic. The ground is colder and warms later than in most places south of Alaska.

In Alaska we have mineral soil and organic soil, although most land will have a mix of the two. Mineral-based soils are clay, silt, sand, and loam. Clay has extremely small particles and hence is poorly aerated. It tends to retain water rather than draining well, but it is often nutrient rich. It's difficult to till and compresses easily when wet. Silt soil also has fine particles though they're not as fine as clay. It tends to be moderately fertile and water retentive. Plant roots need pockets of air to breathe. To improve the aeration and texture of both clay and silt, you need to add decomposed organic matter, also called humus. Sandy soil has the largest particles of the mineral-based soils. It is easy to till but drains rapidly and tends to be nutrient deficient. It can be improved through adding humus, which in this case will increase the water-holding capacity and nutrient level. Loam is the soil type most gardeners desire. It has a good balance of all particle sizes, is moist but well draining, and holds nutrients well. Loam is easy to work *and* the vast majority of plants require its characteristics. Peat is an organic-based soil type often found in boggy areas. Formed from decaying plant matter, it can be used to improve the texture of clay and silt soil.

In addition to the physical structure of your soil, it's important to understand several of its other characteristics. One of these is soil pH—a measure of the relative acidity or alkalinity of your soil. It is plotted on a scale ranging from 1 to 14. Numbers below 7 define acidic soil while those above 7 are alkaline. Seven is neutral. Most Alaska soils are mildly to extremely acidic, falling in the range of 4.0 to 6.8. Fortunately, the vast majority of plants prefer mildly acidic soil. If your soil is highly acidic, you can moderate this *a little* by adding calcium carbonate, commonly marketed as gardeners' lime or dolomite lime. It's unlikely that your soil will be too alkaline, but if it is, an application of sulfur or iron sulfate will help reduce the pH. You can also increase soil acidity by using peat as an organic source. In the long run, however, you will have more success matching plants to the pH you have than trying to change the soil pH in a significant way.

Soil fertility is a measure of the nutrients available to plants. Though there are commercial fertilizers available to increase the nutrient level in soil, I prefer adding composted organic matter to improve fertility and texture simultaneously. In coastal Alaska we benefit from the ready availability of compost products based on fish and seaweed. These offer a broad range of nutrients beneficial to plants. Aged and composted animal manure is also available throughout much of Alaska. Steer, llama, horse, and chicken manure can all be used, but I avoid horse manure as it is often filled with undesirable weed seeds. Others find well-aged horse manure a wonderful source of garden nutrients. The key phrase, though, is *well aged*, meaning composted for several years before using. Neither dog nor cat excrement should be utilized as it can carry parasites and pathogens to which humans are susceptible.

Incorporating organic matter into your garden soil will benefit both soil and plant health by increasing the microorganism community in your soil. These unseen creatures help in a variety of ways, but essentially they increase the availability of nutrients and improve the soil's retention of them. While there are some harmful microorganisms, most are beneficial; some even set up a symbiotic relationship with plants. *Teaming with Microbes*, a comprehensive and well-received book written by Alaskan Jeff Lowenfels, provides enormous detail on microorganisms, the soil food web, and how to use these to benefit your garden.

If you are blessed with easy-to-work loam and are planning a small garden, turning the soil with a fork is an excellent approach. However, if you have clay or silt soil, which is heavy and difficult to work and requires the addition of lots of compost to improve its texture, you may find tilling a more practical option. This is especially true if you plan to create a large garden. If you wish to till and don't have a tiller, you may be able to rent one. Before using a rented or borrowed tiller, be sure to carefully and completely clean it so you do not introduce new weeds into your garden area.

When first establishing a new garden, I generally till. I like to loosen the soil and mix the chopped surface vegetation into it. I recommend that you till down as deeply as your tiller can manage, going back and forth over the area several times in one direction and then at right angles to the first direction. This will give new plants (except woody ornamentals, which will require holes as deep as their root balls) plenty of loose soil under and around them for root expansion. Now amend your new garden's tilled soil according to what you learned from your soil test and analysis. The easiest way to do this is to spread the recommended amount of nutrients and other additives, including a nice layer of compost, evenly over the tilled area. To get an even distribution spread half of your amendments from east to west and the other half from north to south. Then do another pass in each direction with the tiller to evenly incorporate the amendments into your soil.

If you haven't availed yourself of a soil test and do not plan to do so, the universal amendment that will improve soil in nearly every situation is organic matter. The most common way to add this is by adding compost. Compost is dead plant or animal matter that has undergone a decomposition process. Bagged compost is available commercially. Beware of some of the very inexpensive brands; many have a large component of sawdust and are often not fully composted. Locally produced compost available in bulk is an excellent option to consider and is usually much less expensive than bagged compost. As mentioned earlier, I avoid horse manure because viable weed seeds pass straight through horses, ready to germinate in the garden unless it has been sufficiently aged. Another thing to avoid is grass clippings from a lawn that has been treated with persistent herbicides. Finally, of course, you can make your own compost and incorporate it into your garden beds.

This crushed-rock path is bordered on the garden bed side with casually arranged cobble rocks and on the lawn side with vinyl edging.

As much as I enjoy nearly every facet of gardening, I don't like doing things that seem a waste of time. So if I can head off a problem before it arises, I do. One example of this, as discussed in Chapter 6, "Selecting Successful Plants," is picking plants that stay put. With so many wonderful, well-behaved plants available, it's rare that I choose one that's difficult to manage. Gardening, however, is about more than desirable plants. It also has to do with removing weeds.

## Removing Weeds at the Outset

The simplest definition of a weed is a plant growing where you don't want it to grow. Two of the most widespread and difficult to deal with in Alaska are the annoyingly tenacious horsetail (*Equisetum arvense*) and the aggressive and invasive cow parsnip, known locally as pushki (*Heracleum maximum*). We certainly have other native "weeds" and more than enough introduced ones. In some cases the weed seeds already present in your soil, if left unaddressed, will be viable for years to come. Chickweed seeds are a good example of this. Many undesirable plants use multiple strategies to survive and multiply, making them difficult to eradicate. Nonetheless, in order to reduce maintenance in the long term, it is important to deal with the existing weeds and seed bank at the outset.

Several techniques will work, including temporarily covering with black plastic, good old-fashioned digging, as well as what I call till, amend, and cover. Covering with black plastic requires the least amount of physical effort, but it takes some time and is not one hundred percent effective. Preferably in the early spring, when the target plants are just emerging from the ground, hoe off any weeds that have already germinated. Wait another week or more, and then hoe again, being sure each time that you are getting the roots. Next, cover the area from which you wish to eliminate weeds with black plastic. Secure it in place with landscape staples, rocks, lumber, or other items that will weigh the plastic down so it keeps out light and doesn't blow away. The plastic will deny weed plants water and sunlight. Heat from the sun absorbed by the black material elevates the temperature beneath it, causing seeds near the soil's surface to germinate and the resulting seedlings to die from lack of sunlight and moisture. If left on long enough it accelerates the weakening or death of returning perennial weeds. A forty-five-day treatment is usually sufficient for most weed varieties, though not for horsetail, which has roots extending far beneath the surface, or well-established pushki.

Keep in mind that this technique affects only the seeds that are near the surface, so it is important to refrain from disturbing the soil after treatment. If you disturb or till the soil afterwards, you will bring a fresh set of seeds to the surface where they can germinate. Seeds that require sunlight to germinate that hadn't sprouted prior to covering with plastic may sprout after you remove it. If they do, remove them quickly before their root system gets established.

If you plan to add new topsoil to your garden beds to elevate or raise them above the surrounding area, as discussed in Chapter 16, "Building Your Garden Beds," the black plastic technique should work well for you if you layer the new soil on top of the soil you have treated. This technique is also a good choice on grades that are too steep to till.

An alternative and more effective approach is to till, amend, and cover. As in the first method, it's best to do this in spring so you have a minimal amount of weed plant matter with which to contend. You will, however, have to wait for the soil to dry out from the melting snow before tilling. Otherwise you can do real damage to the structure of your soil.

Once your soil has dried sufficiently, deeply till the area to be planted. After tilling, add the amendments suggested by your soil test. Regardless of whatever else you need to add, it is usually a good idea to spread a two- to three-inch layer of compost over the entire area. (See Chapter 14, "Preparing Your Soil," for more details on this subject.) Till all amendments and compost into the soil. Next, do any sculpting or mounding you have planned. Then cover the prepared soil with six to eight layers of newspaper to block out all light and cover the paper with woven geotextile material (Typar) or heavy-duty landscape fabric. Secure it in place with landscape staples, rocks, or other heavy items.

Now, here's the hardest part with this technique—wait a year. Most of us are too impatient to wait this long, but if you do the results will be incredible. When you remove the fabric a year later, you will have a wonderful, weed-free place to plant. Once again, be careful to minimally disturb the treated area so you don't bring any viable seeds to the surface. The till, amend, and cover technique is perfect for multiyear projects and those with a lot of hardscape elements since you can let the weed treatment work while you build your hardscape or develop other beds.

Finally, if your area is small or has a manageable number of weeds, hand digging each individual weed is a reasonable approach. It is important to remove the entire root of each weed; pulling weeds rather than digging them rarely accomplishes the desired result.

When you remove turf grass to make way for a garden bed, digging out the few weeds left behind works well. Take note that removing turf grass before locating a garden bed in a former lawn area is essential. It is fairly easy to do if you dig just below the root level and roll the grass back as you go. Building a garden on top of turf without removing it will produce a long-term maintenance nightmare.

## Low-Maintenance Paths

Paths are an integral part of a garden. In some cases they may cover even more square feet than the garden beds do. Therefore, it's important to construct them so they do not add to the overall maintenance of the landscape.

Drainage and weed abatement must be kept in mind. Because our soils freeze so deeply, water tends to pool at ground level for long periods in spring as we go through

Slate paths are held firmly in place and separated from the bark mulch with Seldovia granite.

Gravel paths benefit from a decorative trim that keeps garden mulch and gravel separated.

breakup. Your paths should be constructed to shed this water by incorporating a slight slope and/or by using permeable material and underlaying the paths with a good drainage medium. It's critical to put a weed barrier beneath the drainage layer. This is one of the welcome instances when the most effective technique is also one of the least expensive. After you excavate for your path, lay down six or eight layers of overlapping newspaper to totally block out light, and then cover it with road-grade Typar. Your drain material goes on top of the weed barrier. Be sure to use the woven, road-grade fabric, not the felt-like septic version. Horsetail grows right through the latter!

There are many material choices for the finish layer of your paths. A practical and easy-to-install choice is gravel. If you have access to crushed rock, you'll find it much more comfortable to walk on than pea gravel or other rounded stones. Natural stone like slate is lovely, but must be laid evenly with reasonably narrow joints for best footing. If you choose bark mulch or spruce needles as a path surface, be sure the surface beneath it is level and nonskid. Mulch can scoot out from underfoot otherwise. Manufactured stone like pavers can also make a nice even path, but as with slate can be somewhat expensive. Both slate and pavers should be laid over a fast-draining material to minimize frost heaving. One of the simplest, but still an interesting and effective path surface, is grass. The choice you make will obviously depend on your budget, but also on the look and style you wish to achieve.

Most path materials require some form of edging on either side of the path to keep the material in place. Crushed rock, gravel, slate, and other natural stone as well as manufactured stone paths will remain tidier if constructed using decorative border material like larger rocks or block laid on edge on either side. Equally functional though not as attractive is basic vinyl or metal edging. If your path is covered with the same material as an adjoining garden bed, no boundary is necessary. This is the case with bark mulch paths through a garden bed top-dressed with bark mulch. Grass paths should *always* be contained with a vertical edging. Turf grass is lovely and provides a wonderful frame for a garden, but it is one of the most aggressive plants we invite into our gardens!

## More on Edging

At all boundaries where grass meets any other element in your landscape except perhaps concrete, use vertical edging to keep the grass in check. Doing this will greatly reduce your maintenance burden. In other parts of the world, like my hometown of Philadelphia, vertical edging may be looked down upon by some. The gardener is instructed to carefully cut a V-shape gap between lawn and the garden bed and redo this periodically during the season. Fine for Outside perhaps, but gardeners there don't contend with twenty hours or more of sunlight during the growing season! If you have access to it, use contractor-grade material that's at least five inches deep and comes in sixteen- or twenty-foot lengths. The material may be vinyl, color-coated aluminum, or steel. Regardless of finish, be sure to stake the edging every four feet or so to hold it in the ground during freeze-thaw cycles. Drive stakes toward the grass at approximately a forty-five-degree angle to the plane of the edging. There is nothing less attractive than vinyl edging sticking up halfway out of the ground; what's more, it's not performing its containment function when not held in place. Grass roots travel laterally from the soil surface to about three inches below it. Your edging must be deep enough to block the roots and still have a bit exposed above the soil level to prevent grass from hopping over the top. Purely functional edging can be used in conjunction with a decorative border such as cobble rocks, slate, or driftwood. To use both, put the decorative border on the garden side of the edging, in other words on the opposite side of the edging from the grass.

One other tip about edging for lower maintenance is shown in the photo on page 101. If you put a few lateral inches of crushed gravel on the opposite side of the edging from your lawn, you can put one wheel of your mower on it as you mow along the

Bark paths within a bark-mulched garden do not require edging of any sort.

garden bed or path. This allows you to mow and trim all at once! If you have a riding mower with wide wheels, make the gravel area ample enough for the wheels to pass without disturbing any decorative treatment you utilize and be sure to keep the turning radius of the mower in mind as you lay out your beds and paths.

## Other Uses for Typar

We've talked about using newspaper and Typar under your paths for weed abatement. This combination can be used to inhibit weeds in other situations as well. If you are carving your garden out of a wild area filled with many Alaska native plants, these tenacious fellows will be continuing sources of weeds in your garden beds. Create a buffer area between the wild vegetation and the more refined areas to diminish this annoyance. Happily, this works two ways: a buffer area will also help protect natural areas from garden plants. Cover a swath six feet or wider between your garden beds

and an undeveloped area with multilayers of newspaper and Typar. Secure it all in place with landscape staples. Cover the geotextile cloth with mulch that matches or coordinates with your garden style and finish. While this technique works in most cases, it may not be sufficient to control aspen and poplar suckers. In this case you may also need to dig a substantial trench beyond the fabric buffer area.

Other applications for this effective weed-barrier treatment include beneath dry streambeds, rock gardens, "fields" of gravel, rock, or mulch, and raised vegetable beds. Be sure to make any perennial beds constructed over Typar *at least* ten inches high so the plant roots have room to spread. Typar and newspaper are also helpful to keep weeds at bay when used behind dry-stacked rock walls.

Though some folks do it, I do *not* recommend using this treatment on top of garden beds. From a practical point of view, once you cut holes into the fabric, you've introduced a light source for the weeds beneath it. A lushly planted garden bed will have enough holes to render the covering totally useless as a weed blocker. When the weeds poke through a hole seeking sunlight, you will find it virtually impossible to get to the root of the unwanted plants. Further, should you wish to move your plants around at a future date, you will have to cut fresh holes each time—a tedious task after years of mulch has accumulated on top of the covering.

Driftwood can be used effectively
in a casual garden.

When creating your garden beds it is enormously helpful to construct them so their soil level is higher than the surrounding ground. This will improve your success for several reasons.

First, raised beds will shed water more quickly during the freeze-thaw-freeze cycles that occur seasonally in northern climates. Without a ready exit from the garden bed, water from melted snow or ice will either refreeze on the soil surface, suffocating the plants below, or remain in its liquid state and rot the crown of the plants immersed in moisture. The easiest way to avoid this discouraging outcome is to elevate the beds above the ground surrounding them. A six-inch differential is usually sufficient. You, of course, can make the garden beds even higher for drama or easier access.

Raising or elevating your garden beds from the area surrounding them is also an effective technique to help warm the soil in the beds earlier in the season. The result is a slightly longer growing season, something we all desire. Raised beds will also help those of you who garden in areas with permafrost by lifting your plants' roots that much higher above the frigid ground below them.

There are many ways to create raised beds. You can simply mound up the soil, letting gravity hold it in place. Alternatively, you can use rocks, driftwood, manufactured block, metal, lumber, concrete, or other material to create a raised structure to contain your garden soil. The choice you make will depend on the style of your garden. You may want to coordinate with hardscape elements you use elsewhere in the landscape, making the structure surrounding your garden beds an integral part of your overall design.

A good example of a garden that will shed water quickly during snowmelt and create a toasty-warm environment for plant roots is a rock garden, a specialty form of raised bed. By their very nature rock gardens provide excellent drainage largely because they are elevated substantially from the area surrounding them. They're also often constructed of fast-draining material—lean sandy soil, gravel, and rock

A steeply mounded island will add drama and dynamism to your design.

Clockwise:

Even concrete can be used to create a well-drained raised bed. Note the soil is mounded within the structure to shed water. The concrete has periodic drain slots as well.

Treated wood timbers make an effective raised bed and low retaining wall.

Both the elevation and material used in rock gardens combine for rapidly draining gardens and a warm environment for plants.

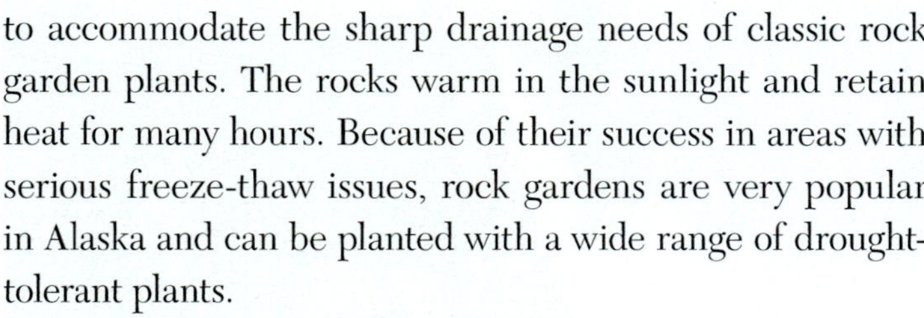

to accommodate the sharp drainage needs of classic rock garden plants. The rocks warm in the sunlight and retain heat for many hours. Because of their success in areas with serious freeze-thaw issues, rock gardens are very popular in Alaska and can be planted with a wide range of drought-tolerant plants.

The topography of sloping ground automatically takes care of draining off most excess moisture. As a result, it's not necessary to raise the planting area on a slope. Conversely, if you have a high water table (water just below the surface of the soil) where you garden, you can improve your success if you raise your beds even higher than six inches so the plant roots will be above the water table.

Two exceptional cases where raised beds are *not* in order are in a bog garden or a rain garden. Both are typically created using plants that thrive in wet, boggy conditions.

Rusted steel can be employed to fashion interesting structures that add color as well as unique texture to the garden.

The slope of a hillside garden naturally sheds water, eliminating the need for a raised bed. South-facing slopes warm earlier than those that are flat or north-facing.

When buying your plants at
the nursery select only healthy
ones. Remember not all insects
are "bad"; some are beneficial.

Most gardeners love buying plants. A nursery is a stimulating place filled with beauty and fragrance. It can take great personal discipline to purchase only what you *plan* to buy. One of the advantages of doing a garden design is that it helps you focus on the plants you've chosen through research and consideration rather than being seduced by what's in bloom. This is not to say it will work one hundred percent, nor should it. After all, gardening is supposed to be fun, so an impulsive purchase of a drop-dead-gorgeous specimen isn't the worst thing that can happen. It certainly happens to me—a lot!

Let's assume, though, that you are at the nursery to purchase the plants in your design. How do you select the best plants from among those offered? There are several things to bear in mind.

Plant health is the most critical issue. Look for foliage that appears fresh, not droopy, and not yellowed (unless of course it's a plant that's supposed to have golden foliage). Look for signs of new growth on the plant. If the plant has multiple stems, the new growth will likely be at the center of the crown, a somewhat mounded area just above soil level. If the plant has a branching structure, look for new shoots along and at the end of the branches. New growth indicates the plant has gotten over the shock of being transplanted into the pot it's in and is beginning to develop again.

Inspect the plant for damaging insects. Avoid plants infested with aphids, spider mites, white flies, or other parasites. Not only do these insects weaken the plant, they may also spread to other plants in your garden when you take them home. Remember not all insects are "bad." Many of our nurseries use beneficial insects rather than sprays to control destructive insects. Most of us recognize every child's favorite, the ladybug (lady beetle) as well as the prehistoric-looking praying mantis. Both of these are beneficial as are lacewings, with which you may be less familiar. If you see insects and are not sure if they are good or bad, ask someone with the nursery. Trust me, if the plant is infested with detrimental insects, the nursery folks will want to know it so they can take action to stop them from spreading throughout their inventory.

Another pest you should inspect for is the ubiquitous slug. On occasion you'll spot one of these on the bottom of a pot that has been sitting on the ground; more often you'll see only the slug damage on the leaves of the plant. Slugs make roundish holes in the foliage. Bypass plants with obvious slug damage; the soil in the pot may contain slugs, which are easy enough to spot, but also slug eggs, which are quite easy to miss. This is a pest that you absolutely do not want to introduce into your garden.

Inspect the surface of the soil in the nursery pots. Are weeds growing in it? If so, you may want to reconsider and select a different plant. Unfortunately, some potting mixes and the soil that comes with field-grown plants can be a source of new weeds— for your garden and for Alaska. In the next chapter, "Planting Techniques," I'll explain a technique to minimize the risk of bringing weeds into your garden when planting, but the first step is to refrain from knowingly buying them.

If you have a choice, select plants that are in bud rather than in bloom. The plant will tolerate moving from its pot to your soil better if it's not trying to support a lot of open flowers. Besides, don't you want to enjoy the blooms *after* the plant goes home with you? You'll get a longer window of pleasure if the plant is still in bud when you buy it.

Finally, take note of how full the plant is in the pot. Look for plants that are lush but not so big that the pot is restricting their growth. If plants are left in the same size pot for too long, their roots begin to circle around the inside of the pot. This condition is often called *root-bound*. While a bit of this can be corrected at planting by untangling and freeing the roots, if the condition is extreme it can cause serious problems long term. This is especially true with shrubs and trees, where root-bound specimens should be avoided.

When selecting trees look for a strong central leader. The leader is the uppermost portion of a major structural limb. In the ideal case, the highest and stoutest leader is the center one—hence the central leader. The leader is the primary growth point for a tree and "leads" the tree upwards. Separate trees or shrubs you are considering from the others so you can carefully examine their shape and structure. You want a tree with well-spaced branches, not one with branches all emanating from the same location on the trunk. Look for a symmetrical shape with a good balance of branches all around the trunk. Bypass trees with a forked main trunk; these may split with maturity or snow weight.

Trees are often priced by the diameter (caliper) of their trunks, though sometimes they are priced by the size of the pot. If your nursery uses the latter method, choose the tree with the largest caliper, all other things being equal. Avoid trees with damaged bark. Shrubs should also be symmetrical and have nice branching and a pleasing shape.

Because our climate can be somewhat challenging to new plants, it's best to select the largest plants you can possibly afford. That is, if the nursery offers the same variety of perennial in a four-inch and six-inch pot, purchase the six-inch size. If a given shrub is available in a one-gallon or five-gallon pot, take the five-gallon one. The larger the pot and plant, the more mature the plant should be. Purchasing mature, healthy plants will increase your success rate considerably in our challenging environment.

If you want your plants to mingle,
plant them slightly closer than
their expected mature size.

t's time to plant! Up until now all the planning and hard work has been a preamble to your ultimate goal of creating a successful and beautiful garden. Putting the plants into the ground will finally make your garden come to life.

Assuming you have fully prepared the areas for the new purchases you've just brought home from the nursery, it's best to get them planted as soon as you can. If you're not quite ready, keep your plants in a shady area away from the intensity of afternoon sun. Most nursery pots are black or dark green and will absorb a tremendous amount of heat if the sun shines on them for any length of time. Many perennials, trees, and shrubs that do well in our cool climate can be damaged or die from their roots getting too hot. Direct sunlight will also quickly dry out potting soil, increasing the need for frequent watering. In any case, be sure your plants are well hydrated before you begin the planting process.

When it's time to move forward, you'll need a shovel or trowel and a large bucket lined with a lawn-and-leaf bag. You may also want to have a kneeling pad or knee pads so you'll be more comfortable as you work. Always try to kneel or stand *outside* the boundaries of the garden bed. If it's too wide for you to reach all of it from outside, stay on stepping-stones or maintenance paths placed within the bed so you don't compact your soil in the areas designated for planting.

As you pick up each plant, inspect it one more time for pests, removing any that you see before placing it in the garden bed. Handpick and discard slugs. Aphids and other sucking insects can be removed by holding the pot upside down or laying it on its side and spraying the foliage with a strong stream of water. Spray all the foliage and stems, but give particular attention to spraying the undersides of the foliage where aphids concentrate. Do this away from the garden bed.

Remove any discolored or damaged foliage and put it into the bucket. Doing this before situating the plant in the garden ensures it will look its best, but more important, you'll be alerted to a potential problem if discoloration or damage presents itself thereafter.

With your plan and a tape measure in hand, place your pots in a garden bed according to the spacing you've determined on your detailed plan. If you have large or heavy trees and shrubs, you may wish to use a placeholder for these until you have made all your adjustments and are sure of their locations. An empty bucket or surveyor's stake will do nicely. When you're finished laying out everything, stand back and look at the arrangement from all viewing directions to be sure you're satisfied with

how it will look. Try to envision the plants as they will grow to maturity and make any necessary adjustments before you begin the actual digging.

Now, while holding the pot and plant over your large bucket, remove about a quarter inch of soil from the top, letting it fall into the lined bucket. Then carefully slip out the root ball and discard a half inch or so of soil from the bottom, adding it to the bucket as well. The reason for removing the soil is to avoid introducing pests into the garden—many damaging insects lay their eggs on the surface of the soil while slugs lay their eggs at the bottom, often near the drain holes. Carefully inspect the soil around the sides of the root for slug eggs and remove them. Slug eggs are small, whitish orbs that look a lot like tapioca and are usually present in clusters. The eggs are similar in size to some time-release fertilizers but are translucent while fertilizers are usually opaque.

With the exception of a few plants that resent having their roots handled (columbine and poppies in particular) loosen any circling roots. Dig a hole that is two times wider than the root ball and the same depth as the root ball is tall. If you've prepared and amended your soil as discussed earlier, there is no need for additional amendments at planting time. (If you haven't prepared your soil, then add a couple of handfuls of compost to the soil excavated from the planting hole. Mix the two together before backfilling the hole.)

Set the plant into the hole, rotating it so its best face is positioned toward the primary viewing location. Check to ensure that the crown of the plant will be at the same level relative to the soil surface as it was in the nursery pot. Add or remove soil from the bottom of the hole as necessary. Backfill the hole around the root ball with the excavated soil and pat it firmly into place. If you are planting a tree, a shrub, or even a perennial with a particularly large root structure, pause after you've filled the hole about halfway. Add enough water to top off the remaining space in the excavation. After the water soaks in, finish adding soil to the planting hole. Press the soil snugly around the plant to ensure good root contact.

As soon as you finish installing a given bed, water it deeply before moving on to the next major section. Tie up the lawn-and-leaf bag with the discarded soil and damaged foliage and take it to the landfill. Do *not* put this refuse onto your compost pile.

Bark offers a nice contrast to
rock and slate.

Mulch is a material used to top-dress your garden. (The same word is used to describe an additional layer added to a garden bed in the fall to insulate and protect your plants in winter. We'll discuss the latter use of mulch in the next chapter, "Weeds and Other Maintenance.") Mulch used as a top-dressing serves four purposes: (1) it conserves moisture, reducing the frequency of watering; (2) it stops rain from splashing mud onto the foliage of the plants; (3) it assists a little in weed suppression and removal, though unless it's at least four inches thick, it does not completely suppress weeds; and (4) mulch also provides a cosmetic finishing touch to the appearance of the landscape. In some cases it eventually helps to build the humus content of the soil and may also acidify soils over time.

The options available to you are quite diverse. They include finely shredded bark (usually called bark mulch), chunky pieces of bark (sometimes referred to as beauty bark), gravel of varying sizes, rock chips or shavings, sand, grass clippings and chopped leaves, colored rocks, ground glass pieces, recycled tire rubber, and more. Each has its pros and cons.

Mulch will retain moisture and helps with weed abatement.

Bark mulch softens the hard surfaces of this modern hospital and adds to the quiet atmosphere of the "Serenity Garden."

Bark mulch can be used on paths within a mulched garden bed if you want to keep the focus on the plants rather than the path.

Bark mulch is excellent for moisture retention and average for weed suppression. It's fairly inexpensive and easy to apply. Over the course of a year its color will gray so it needs to be lightly refreshed each spring to look its best. Cosmetically, bark is effective in woodland and naturalistic settings. It softens the look of a garden constructed with a lot of masonry. It will, over time, break down and add to the humus content of your soil.

Beauty bark, the large chunky bark, serves only a cosmetic purpose. The pieces don't interlock well, so it does little to conserve moisture or assist with weeds. It takes more volume to cover an area than it would with bark mulch, effectively making it more expensive. It

Gravel mulch warms the soil in this simple rose garden.

Rock gardens are an ideal environment for gravel mulch.

doesn't break down for a number of years, but will gray over the winter. If you have a thick enough layer you can turn the bark to reveal a brighter side each spring for a few years, but ultimately you'll need to add fresh material to keep it looking attractive.

Gravel and rock chips used as mulch help warm the soil by absorbing the sun's heat, making them ideal options for cold Alaska soils. A thick layer of rock will assist with weed abatement and moisture retention. Some gardeners find gravel difficult to clean up in spring and think it traps weed seeds. This hasn't been my experience. It may take a little more attention during spring cleaning than bark, but I find its warming capacity to be so beneficial as to outweigh that concern. Because gravel doesn't break down, it rarely needs refreshing. It's a natural choice for rock gardens and also works well in cottage gardens. When applying rock mulch on a sloping garden, press it firmly into the soil to hold it from sliding downhill. Gravel is a fairly inexpensive option.

Sand is a fun choice in a beach-themed garden. It holds moisture, absorbs heat, and is inexpensive. If you gather sand from the beach, it's a good idea to wash it to remove salts. Over the years sand will work its way into the soil so it will need periodic refreshment.

Grass clippings and chopped leaves are plentiful and usually free. They are good insulators so can be employed as temporary protective winter mulch. A thin layer can serve as a simple cosmetic treatment. Both grass and leaves will break down during the course of the year so they will need to be reapplied annually. Be careful to avoid grass clippings from lawns that have weeds, have been sprayed with herbicides, or are not mowed regularly. In the last case you may inadvertently add grass seed from early-blooming short grasses to your garden bed.

Colored rocks, ground glass, and recycled tire rubber are available but tend to be much more expensive than natural products. Used in small doses the first two can be quite effective accents, but they can distract from the beauty of your plants when used to cover large areas. Recycled tire mulch brings the potential of chemical leaching and is, in my opinion, too insulating for our climate. While all of the other mulch options discussed have their merits and should be selected based on your taste and garden design, I do not recommend the use of rubber mulches.

Regardless of the type of mulch you choose, in Alaska it's best to apply it sparingly. Most forms of mulch are somewhat insulating. In hot climates, gardeners often pile on a thick layer to keep soils cool. In northern climates, we have the opposite issue—our soils are incredibly cold. We want them to warm as soon as possible in spring. For us, it's better to have a thin layer of mulch so the warmth of the sun can penetrate it to heat the ground. The exceptions are gravel or rock chip mulches, which will absorb the sun's heat and transfer it to the soil. In that case a thick layer is just fine.

Use a range of gravel sizes to create a naturalistic look.

This garden was full of all sorts of weeds and had become a burden rather than a pleasure for its owner. There was a barely noticeable but nice tree that deserved salvaging. Little else was worth digging up and cleaning. The solution was to cover the entire garden with newspaper and geotextile fabric and build a rock garden on top to complement the one to the right.

The result is an easy-care rock garden planted with a color palette similar to the existing one on the right. Now the owner can sit on her bench and enjoy the refurbished garden and the view. An added bonus is that without all the competition from weeds, the salvaged tree is now thriving.

There are about as many definitions of weeds as there are gardeners. Plants cultivated with pleasure in one part of the country may be considered a nuisance in another. Perhaps the simplest definition of a weed is a plant that *insists* on growing where you do not want it to grow.

Sometimes plants that are considered weeds when they appear uninvited in a garden are part of the local indigenous flora. They have adapted well to their home base and when we disturb the soil to change nature's work, we often find these locals to be much more tenacious than the plants we introduce. In Alaska, we have our fair share of these rugged specimens, many of which employ multiple methods of propagation. They can set an enormous number of seeds, send out runners or rhizomes to establish new colonies, and/or grow long, delicate roots that break off easily, leaving enough behind to sprout again. Some native plants have roots that are so big that use of a pickax is your only hope of removing them completely.

To keep a garden weed-free, consistent periodic weeding is a must. We can prepare a new bed to rid ourselves of the initial presence of weeds, as described in Chapter 14, "Preparing Your Soil," but wind-borne seeds will drift into the gardens each fall. Birds and other creatures will drop seeds of plants we don't want precisely where we don't want them. New topsoil we purchase as well as amendments we add will occasionally bring weeds with them. Plants we choose to put into our gardens may create more seedlings than we want. As a result, to keep your garden looking its best, it's important to weed early and often.

When annual weed seedlings first sprout, their root systems are small, making them easy to remove. Always try to get the entire root. Perennial weeds like dandelions may have a more substantial root, but the same rule applies—endeavor to get all of it. With some plants, like horsetail, this is nearly impossible, as their roots travel several feet belowground. However, based on some experiments done by Alaska's peony farmers, we've learned that if you diligently cut or pull off its green top as soon as it sprouts, you'll eventually win the battle with horsetail by weakening the entire root system.

With a new garden properly prepared, you shouldn't have many weeds. From that point on vigilance is the key. Do not let unwanted plants get established. A trick I've used successfully for years is to keep a small hand trowel tucked into each garden bed so it's handy whenever I spot a weed. I use trowels with either green or black handles so they become "invisible." Having a proper tool nearby allows me to remove a weed completely as soon as I spot it.

If you remove weeds regularly you won't need to worry about their multiplying by going to seed. This is critical. *Never* let weeds go to seed in your garden! That would bring to naught all of the hard work you put into preparing your garden beds and turn a small task, when done in a timely manner, into an enormous one.

## What If Your Garden Is Already Full of Weeds?

But what if you're learning these techniques too late and you already have weeds and their seeds in your garden beds? How can you regain control? Depending on how bad your situation is, there are several options, but they all take effort and time—both hours and years. If you have several garden beds and feel overwhelmed, break the task into manageable pieces. Get one bed restored. You'll see how much better it looks and learn how much easier it is to care for once you've corrected your problem. This experience will give you the confidence and optimism to continue to the next bed and the next until you have finished the project.

Start with the bed on the most windward side of your property (the side from which wind comes) and carefully and thoroughly dig out each weed. Take your time and do each section right. Haphazard weeding, removing some but not all, or neglecting to get at the roots is *nearly* a waste of time. Worse, it will discourage you. For example, chickweed seems easy to remove, right? You just grab a handful, give a pull, and it's out. Wrong. Unfortunately, you've left the root behind and it will produce a new plant in nothing flat. If you slow down and carefully follow the extraordinarily fine, thread-like stalk to the ground, pursue it into the soil with your trowel and pop out the root, you will have accomplished something. Throw the exhumed plant into a bucket lined with a trash bag. Later you will take the bag to the landfill. Continue through the first bed until you have finished it. Now stay diligent and remove new weeds as soon as they sprout.

If your garden has been weedy for an extended amount of time, your soil will have a large store of unwanted seeds in it. Many of these will be viable for years. Each spring and fall will bring a flush of new plants from these seeds. Fortunately, if you get after them as soon as they appear they will be easy to remove completely.

Preemergent agents, like corn gluten, inhibit the germination of seeds and may be of some help in extreme cases. They will *not* kill existing plants. They act by desiccating seeds so the seeds are no longer viable. Preemergents are indiscriminate, however, so if you have desirable self-sowers in your garden, their seeds will be affected as well. These products must be reapplied periodically and have mixed reviews among northern gardeners, but they may help you.

If your situation is severe and especially if good plants are infested with weeds, you may need to take a more drastic approach, essentially starting over. On a cool day dig up the plants you want to salvage. Put them into a wheelbarrow of water and thoroughly remove the soil from each plant's roots. You can do this by swishing the plant back and forth in the water. As with weeding, you must do a thorough job to accomplish your goal. Remove all the soil to ensure you have removed all the unwanted seeds. Now carefully look at the roots of your plant. If the plant is infested with a weed, careful examination will let you see which roots belong to the good plant and which belong to an unwanted resident. Remove the latter. If the plant needs dividing, this is a good time to do that too. In fact, dividing the plant may make it easier to remove unwanted weeds. Pot up the cleaned plant in some soilless potting mix, water it, and set it in the shade while you continue the project. Repeat this process until each plant you wish to salvage has been carefully treated.

Next you will address the garden bed and its weedy soil. Using the labor-saving technique of covering and waiting a year as discussed earlier is probably not an option unless you have a weed-free home for your salvaged plants. The extent of your problem and whether your most troublesome weeds propagate by seed or spread by root and rhizome will lead you to one of two approaches.

If you have root spreaders or preside over a horsetail "forest," you can give up on the old soil, cover the bed with newspaper and Typar, add a foot of topsoil, and replant.

A less drastic approach for seed spreaders is to remove the top three or so inches of soil (where the majority of weed seeds will reside), cover the remaining soil with a thick layer of newspaper but no fabric, and then put six to eight inches of amended commercial-grade topsoil on top of the paper. The paper will block light from any remaining weed seeds. Over time it will break down and allow plant roots to penetrate it. Replant your salvaged plants and add new ones as you choose. The following photos provide an example of the kind of results this approach can accomplish.

Do not leave weeds on the ground after digging them, as chickweed seeds and those of many other weeds will mature and germinate even though the plant has been dug up. Stem pieces left in the garden may root so take care to remove all weed litter. Never put weeds in your compost pile for the same reason. Theoretically, a well-tended compost pile will heat up enough to kill most seeds, but how many of us

Lovely native iris (*Iris setosa*) and dainty shooting stars (*Dodecatheon pulchellum ssp. pauciflorum*) struggled to survive in this garden hidden among a throng of aggressive weeds.

really monitor our compost carefully enough to be sure this has happened? Not me. So why take the chance?

As summer wanes and the indigenous plants near your garden begin to set seed, you can take steps to reduce your spring weeding by deadheading some of the worst seed producers. For me the big evildoer is pushki. Lovely as its flowers might be, it is extremely aggressive and thrives on the extra water a garden or lawn nearby affords it. Unchecked, pushki will take over. So I enjoy their show and then, covering myself from head to foot to avoid getting the burns their sap can cause on my skin, I go into the fields surrounding my garden and deadhead every one I see.

## Other Maintenance

Each year your garden needs to be cut back in either fall or spring. Herbaceous perennials (those that die back to the ground during freezing weather), ferns, and some grasses will go dormant as winter approaches. At some point their spent foliage needs to be removed to make way for fresh spring growth. Some folks prefer to cut their gardens back in fall and to remove the foliage at that time so their gardens will be neat and tidy when spring arrives; others prefer to let the spent foliage remain on the plants to provide an insulating layer for the plant roots and crown. There are excellent and knowledgeable gardeners in each camp. I prefer to leave the foliage until spring for insulation and so that I can enjoy every last minute of my garden until it disappears under winter's snow. A gardening friend likes to leave her perennials in the garden until spring so she can enjoy their attractive seedpods. The flower stalks of the daylilies that line her driveway also serve as guides to show the snowplow the edge of her garden!

Whether you attend to this gardening house-keeping in spring or fall, peonies should always be cut back *to the ground* in fall because they are susceptible to a fungal disease called botrytis blight or gray mold (*Botrytis paeoniae* and *B. cinerea*) that can live on their foliage and in their stems through the winter. Because of the potential for this disease, peony foliage should never be put onto your compost pile. Some folks also choose to cut back delphiniums and lilies in the fall even if they do the rest of their cleanup in spring. Although I deadhead lilies so the plant's energy nourishes the bulbs rather than forming seeds, I choose not to cut back delphiniums.

Whenever you cut back other than peony plants, do not cut too closely to the crown of the plant. Grasses in particular resent close cutting. Some grasses should not be cut back at all but rather have their spent foliage teased out of the clump by combing through the foliage with your fingers in spring—blue fescue (*Festuca glauca*) and blue oat grass (*Helictotrichon sempervirens*) are two of these. The spent foliage of disease-free and pest-free plants can be composted for addition to your garden at a later time.

The remedy was to dig up and carefully clean the valued plants, remove the top three inches of weedy soil, put down a thick layer of newspaper, top that with eight inches of quality top soil, and then replant. Now the salvaged plants flourish in their weed-free environment.

Gardens benefit immensely from an annual application of compost each spring. After the garden is cleaned up, add compost to the soil surface around each plant if your garden is sparsely planted or over the entire bed if your plants are close together. Some folks pull their mulch away from the plant before adding compost and then push the mulch back into place. Alternatively, if your compost is quite fine you can sprinkle it on top of your mulch and water it in. In either case the compost will work its way into the soil throughout the season, providing a continuous source of organic nutrients.

When you water your garden it's best to water deeply and infrequently rather than sparingly every couple of days. If you water deeply, your plants will adapt and seek moisture by sending their roots down into the soil, making them more drought tolerant. Frequent shallow watering will encourage a shallower root structure, making

Consistent winter-long snow cover makes excellent mulch. This photo was taken on April 11.

the plant more susceptible to drought and possibly winter kill. Instead of adhering to a regular schedule for watering (every seven days, for example), take rain into account and check the moisture content of your soil a few inches down to see if watering is necessary. As you water, weed, or stroll through your garden, look for pests and problems as you go. Infestations and diseases caught early are much easier to correct than those left unattended for a longer period.

We've already discussed protecting your garden from moose, but there are other critters that enjoy the fruits of our efforts. Rabbits love tender young sprouts and snowshoe hares will eat the bark of trees and shrubs. Cyclical surges in the hare population have caused some gardeners to wrap their tree trunks in hardware mesh or other fine-gauge wire during the winter to protect them. If you do this, be sure to remove it during the growing season so the tree's growth is not restricted by the wire. Porcupines can decimate food crops of all sorts. They seem to have a particular penchant for raspberries and broccoli. You can choose to share your crop or try a live trap. If you take the latter path, please release the animal in an area with plenty of cover and *not* near another gardener's home.

Winter winds can be quite desiccating for our woody plants, especially evergreens. It's important to continue to water the garden until the ground freezes solid so your plants are well hydrated going into winter. If you have an especially windy area or plants that are marginally hardy, you may want to consider erecting a wind block, spraying with a product like Wilt-Pruf, or wrapping conifers in burlap to minimize dehydration.

In fall you may also want to mulch your gardens with a thick layer of grass clippings, shredded leaves, or spruce boughs to protect perennials and woody plants from intensely cold winters. Use grass clippings that are free of herbicides and weeds. Also, avoid leaves from trees infested with unwanted garden pests. Birch trees often suffer from aphids or leaf miners, so inspect them carefully before using their foliage as mulch. To shred leaves gather them into a pile and mow them. Regardless of what material you use as an insulating mulch, wait until the ground is frozen to apply it. Then remove it in spring after the freeze-thaw cycle subsides. Snow is wonderfully insulating "mulch." If you garden in an area with *dependable* snow cover throughout the winter and early spring, additional mulching is probably unnecessary.

Have a seat and relax. Remember, a garden is for pleasure. You've earned it, so enjoy it.

Gardens are for pleasure. They are places that delight all our senses with their beauty, fragrances, sounds, textures, and even tastes. They are an art form that is ever-changing both throughout the season and as the years go by. If we let them, gardens can provide moments of serendipity with surprising combinations created by an unanticipated seedling. They bring birds, bees, and butterflies to us. They also attract moose which, though sometimes destructive, are enormously fascinating to watch.

Some gardens are intended as places of refuge and relaxation where we can steal away with a good book or take a few moments to center ourselves. Others may serve as a place to entertain and to be with friends and family. All offer us opportunities to learn and discover new things and to teach our children about nature's wonders. Their purpose is to bring us joy in many ways.

So, please, do allow your garden to give you these gifts. Enjoy it while working in it, but enjoy it as well when you aren't. Walk in your garden. Sit in it. Absorb all the beauty, the smells, and sights you've created. Focus on what's perfect and at times let the things that might be improved upon fade into the background. There will always be something you want to change, but learn to let those thoughts go on occasion so you can revel in what you've created. In short, enjoy your garden!

# Some of My Favorite Hardy Plants and What Makes Them Special

Many Alaska gardens greet spring with the bright yellow blossoms of easy-care globeflowers (*Trollius europaeus*). These delightful plants are also available as a later-blooming orange-flowered species, *Trollius chinensis*, and a dwarf species called *Trollius pumilus*.

While those of us who garden in the Far North may not enjoy the overwhelming number and variety of plants available to gardeners in more temperate climates, we certainly have more than enough options to create compellingly beautiful gardens in whatever style and color scheme we choose. Furthermore, our mild summer climate gives us the opportunity to grow some wonderful plants that struggle in the lower latitudes and to do it with ease—Himalayan blue poppies, primroses, and delphiniums, to name a few. A healthy clump of any one of these three in your garden will generate lots of plant envy among gardeners who toil in sweltering summers. So let's celebrate what we can grow well, try plants from similar latitudes around the globe, and explore interesting choices that other Alaska gardeners are growing with success.

Because the primary purpose of this book is to help you create beautiful, healthy, and well-designed gardens in Alaska and the Far North, I think it's important to talk specifically about how to evaluate a particular plant from a *design* perspective. Given that it will be successful in your environment and fits your color scheme, what makes one plant a better choice than another? Let's explore the plant attributes you should consider when working to create a compelling design.

Look for plants with incredibly long bloom times. An extensive period of flowering makes the whole subject of bloom succession easier when you use some stalwarts that just keep on blooming. Seek options that will extend the season's enjoyment by offering their floral displays extremely early in the year or very late in the season. Our growing season is short; plants with these characteristics will help you have a longer period of pleasure from your garden. So will plants that have brilliant fall foliage or sparkling berries and attractive seed heads. Textured and colorful stems and bark also enhance the garden for extended periods. Consider selections that have spectacular foliage or interesting architectural structures. These attributes will last the entire season and will help you create focal points and dramatic variety in your combinations, making the garden interesting even when little is in bloom. Many plants perfume the air with lovely fragrances or invite

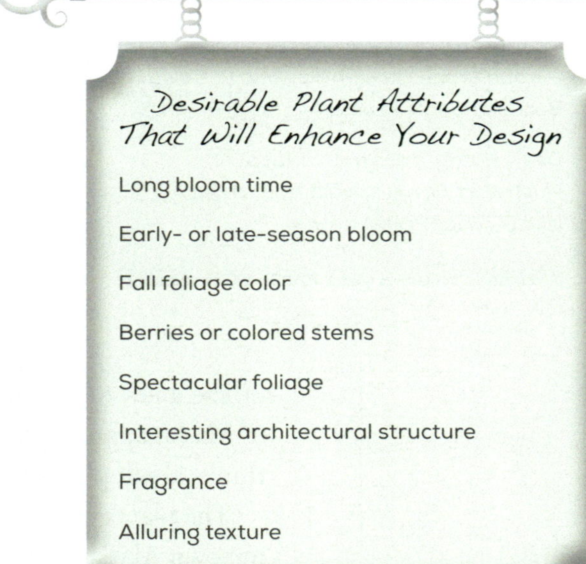

us to touch them with their alluring texture. Both of these qualities will add interest to your design by engaging more of your senses.

From a practical point of view, using well-behaved and easy-care plants will make maintenance much easier. Many plants are tolerant of a broad range of environmental conditions—soil type, moisture level, and light. Plants of this sort will help you avoid inadvertent mismatches between your growing environment and the needs of the plant.

There are several books available with comprehensive plant lists along with detailed descriptions of the horticultural needs of each selection. These books provide information about plants appropriate to your zone and other growing conditions. Rarely will they address how to use the plants to enhance your design efforts.

In order to assist you in taking what you learn about a plant from your research in these books, on the Internet, or even from plant labels and applying it to your design in creative ways, this section will explain how I evaluate and utilize a few of my favorite plants. It is not my intention to offer a comprehensive list of Alaska-appropriate plants but rather to help you see how a designer evaluates and thinks about plants by offering some examples.

The plants included in this section are all ones I have grown successfully in either my own Alaska gardens or those of my clients. Beyond that, each has several attributes that make it stand apart from the crowd. Many deserve much wider use than they currently enjoy. And every one is a favorite of mine because it is special in a garden setting.

In the narrative about each example you'll learn the plant's special attributes, some of the ways you can use it in your designs, as well as minor drawbacks it might have. While some of these may not work in your specific environment, it is my hope the examples will help you consider plants that will thrive in your location from a new and more comprehensive perspective.

In addition to each description is a quick reference box to help you determine if a specific plant will be suitable for your environment. Alaska bloom times are included to aid you as you plan your bloom succession. The first zone number listed is the

---

### Excellent Books with Extensive Plant Lists

*The American Horticultural Society A-Z Encyclopedia of Garden Plants* edited by Christopher Brickell and Judith D. Zuk (DK Publishing, Inc.)

*Herbaceous Perennial Plants* by Allan M. Armitage (University of Georgia Press)

*Rodale's Illustrated Encyclopedia of Perennials* by Ellen Phillips and C. Colston Burrell (Rodale Press)

*Dirr's Hardy Trees and Shrubs: An Illustrated Encyclopedia* by Michael A. Dirr (Timber Press)

coldest USDA zone I've been able to confirm in which the plant has regularly succeeded. If this differs from what is most often seen in the literature, I've included the "official" zone within parentheses following my experience-based number. The zone listed in the literature is often more conservative as very few plants are tested in climates as cold as ours. Most of the following plants appreciate mildly acidic soil; the few exceptions are noted. The plants are listed first by botanical name, followed by one or more of their common names.

*Aconitum x cammarum* 'Bicolor' is both bold and strongly vertical.

### *Aconitum x cammarum* 'Bicolor'
'Bicolor' Monkshood

This elegant, showy, long-blooming hybrid perennial is related to our much more demure native monkshood (*Aconitum delphinifolium* ssp. *delphinifolium*). If you love delphiniums but hate staking, this may be the plant for you as it stands unaided to more than four feet tall. Its relatively narrow girth makes 'Bicolor' monkshood useful as a strong vertical element in the garden. Rather than consigning this selection to the back of the border with other tall plants, you might try placing its narrow profile more forward in your garden bed design scenario to create a bold accent and to break the horizontal plane of midsize plants. Buds are chartreuse, opening to striking hood-shaped blue-and-white clusters liberally arrayed along the top half of stout stems. This mix of colors in a single plant can serve to smoothly transition from one color scheme to the next within the garden and gives you lots of flexibility in your plant combinations. Deeply cut, almost lacy foliage appears delicate and offers a nice contrast to bold-leaved garden partners. Equally at home in sun and part shade, this eye-catching plant does have a drawback—its sap can irritate the skin and the plant and roots are toxic.

Other hardy monkshoods worthy of consideration include common monkshood (*Aconitum napellus*), which is a lovely deep indigo blue, approximately four feet tall, and somewhat bushier in appearance than *Aconitum x cammarum* 'Bicolor.' *Aconitum lamarckii* (which can be seen in the background of the photo opposite) has pale, soft yellow flowers. It grows to more than five feet tall, but needs staking or a stout neighbor on which to lean. Less commonly available is a sweet dwarf variety that stands a mere twelve inches and puts forth similar purply-blue flowers.

> Full sun to part shade
>
> Humus-rich, well-drained, mildly acidic soil
>
> Blooms late July to early September
>
> Height 48", Width 12"
>
> Zone 3

*Aconitum napellus* with 'Summerwine' yarrow (*Achillea millefolium* 'Summerwine').

Above: The subtle interplay of the rich foliage of *Actaea simplex* 'Hillside Black Beauty' and the delicate purple blossoms of candelabra primroses (*Primula alpicola* var. *violacea*) in the foreground enhance the impact of both plants.

Bottom left: Kamchatka bugbane (*Actaea simplex* 'Hillside Black Beauty') contributes to a dark-hued theme in this woodland setting.

Bottom right: Dark-leaved *Actaea simplex* 'Hillside Black Beauty' in the left foreground has wonderfully attractive foliage.

## *Actaea simplex* (formerly *Cimicifuga simplex*)
### Kamchatka Bugbane, Autumn Snakeroot

*Actaea simplex* 'Hillside Black Beauty,' my favorite cultivar of this species, has spectacular, delicately cut, dark-chocolate foliage with an infusion of purple in the hue. Its tall stems are even darker. If the season is long and warm enough, flower spikes covered in tiny white blooms with just a hint of mauve soar above the foliage in September. They look a bit like wispy bottlebrushes, but are much more enticing. Even though the flowers are attractive, the primary reason for including this plant in your garden is its incredible foliage and regal bearing. You can use its color as a backdrop to highlight the delicate blossoms of a nearby plant. It also provides an arresting contrast with pale-green, silver-blue, or variegated foliage like the variegated dogwood shrub (*Cornus alba* 'Elegantissima'). It's a great tool for repetition of a color theme as shown with the dark alder bark below.

Kamchatka bugbane, as this plant is commonly called, is tall and stands erect without support. It is an easy-care plant, but does prefer rich, moist soil for best results. *Actaea simplex* 'Black Negligee' and *Actaea simplex* 'Brunette' have similar eye appeal, though in my experience they are not nearly as vigorous or hardy as *Actaea simplex* 'Hillside Black Beauty.' The roots of all are poisonous.

Part shade to full shade

Humus-rich, moist, acidic soil

Blooms September to October

Height 48", Width 30"

Zone 3

## *Alchemilla mollis*
### Lady's Mantle

Lady's mantle has magnificent foliage. The lobed leaves are covered top and bottom with soft, nearly invisible hairs that make the leaves irresistible to touch. Even better, this fuzzy covering captures and holds dew and raindrops on the surface where they glisten like little diamonds. It is an enchanting thing to see. Fortunately, with our frequent precipitation, we are graced with this experience often! The leaves are a nice size, delicately toothed along the edge and somewhat pleated. While the foliage is truly wonderful and an excellent contrast for lacy or tiny-leaved plants, the sprays of tiny chartreuse flowers held just above the leaves add an enticing frothiness to the overall picture. The flowers have a long vase life and serve as nice filler in bouquets.

> Full sun to part shade
>
> Tolerates most soil types from dry to moist, though not boggy
>
> Blooms mid- to late summer
>
> Height 24", Width 30" or more
>
> Zone 3 (officially Zone 4)

Lady's mantle is a good complement to blues and purples, as can be seen in the photo above, but it works equally well with red, burgundy, orange, chocolate, fuchsia, and white. This versatility makes it a welcome member of nearly every garden design. *Alchemilla mollis* is especially effective as an edging along a path or massed under a stand of trees. It can serve as a neutral color to help you transition from one color scheme to the next or just present a "pretty face" in your garden.

Though this plant will self-sow a bit, most babies are found close to the mother plant and are easy to remove or transplant. Alternatively, deadheading or cutting the flowers for bouquets will eliminate the issue altogether. *Alchemilla mollis* will develop into a large clump. Situate it with plenty of room to grow.

Dew glistens on the exceptional foliage of *Alchemilla mollis*.

Decked out in its frothy flowers, lady's mantle (*Alchemilla mollis*) edges a garden billowing with color and motion.

*Astrantia major* 'Hadspen's Blood.'

A soft pink masterwort is delightful with indigo monkshood (*Aconitum napellus*) (design by Teena Garay).

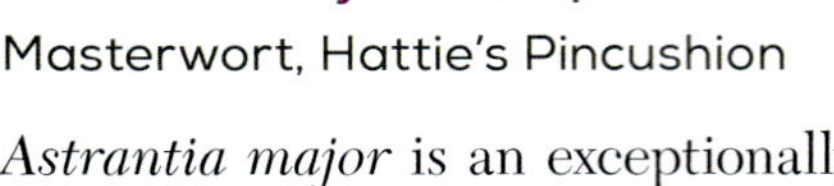

### *Astrantia major* 'Hadspen Blood'
**Masterwort, Hattie's Pincushion**

*Astrantia major* is an exceptionally lovely and versatile perennial species well adapted to Alaska's climate. It offers one of the longest bloom times of any hardy perennial, flowering nonstop from mid-June until Labor Day without any need for deadheading. This plant is covered with masses of perky, one-and-a-half-inch-wide flowers surrounded by star-shaped bracts. Blooms are arrayed in small clusters atop sturdy stems that stand erectly to three feet tall. Foliage is fairly bold, very lush, dark green, deeply toothed, and palm shaped. This exceptional foliage makes a good foil for small-leaved plants while its deeply cut shape serves equally well as a contrast to either sword-shaped foliage like that of iris or bolder-leaved plants like hosta. *Astrantia major* has such a strong presence in the garden that it makes a terrific focal point yet it also blends beautifully in combination with other plants. Its versatility extends to the vase where its cut flowers will look fresh for well over two weeks in water and maintain its color nicely in dried arrangements. Look at the flowers carefully and you'll see why one of the common names for this plant is Hattie's pincushion. It is also called masterwort.

A two-year-old clump of *Astrantia major* 'Star of Beauty' blends well with sea holly (*Eryngium x zabellii* 'Big Blue') and 'Bicolor' monkshood (*Aconitum x cammarum* 'Bicolor') in South Peninsula Hospital's Serenity Garden.

This stately plant forms a fine focal point in a mixed garden.

**Full sun to part shade to shade**

Prefers humus-rich, moisture-retentive, mildly acidic soil

Blooms mid-June to September

Height 24–36", Width 18–30"

Zone 3 (officially Zone 5)

Plants gradually increase in girth, becoming as full as they are tall, but this trouble-free beauty requires no dividing to maintain vigor. At our northern latitudes *Astrantia major* will do best in full sun, but it is also happy in part shade and even full shade, although in the last case it will begin blooming much later. Flower color ranges from deep burgundy to pink to nearly white depending on variety. While 'Hadspen Blood' is my preferred choice, there are many excellent dark red to maroon cultivars (cultivated varieties) of *Astrantia major*: 'Claret,' 'Lars,' 'Moulin Rouge,' and 'Ruby Wedding.' 'Tickled Pink' is, you guessed it, pink.

### *Dicentra eximia*

Fern Leaf Bleeding Heart

This is a lovely alternative to the classic old-fashioned bleeding heart (*Dicentra spectabilis*). The fern leaf cultivars, especially 'Luxuriant' and the more recently introduced 'Candy Hearts,' 'King of Hearts,' and 'Ivory Hearts,' bloom profusely nearly all season with no deadheading necessary. You'll want to plant this selection near the front of your border, along a pathway, or near a sitting area so you can enjoy the sweet heart-shaped flowers of this selection. Its soft, gray-green foliage has an exquisitely delicate texture, making this plant an excellent companion for hosta and other bold-leaved shade plants. Happily, though listed as a shade plant in most literature, it will do just fine in sun at our northern latitudes.

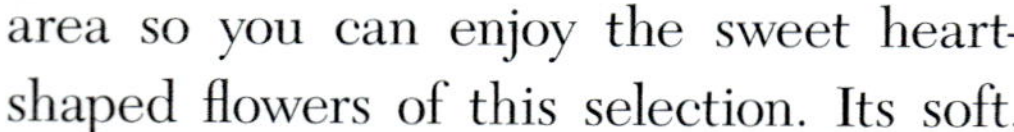

Full sun to full shade

Moist to well-drained, humus-rich soil with pH above 6.8

Blooms mid-June until September

Height 12–15", Width 18"

Zone 3 (officially Zone 4)

Bleeding hearts prefer neutral soil, so this is not a good choice if your soil is highly acidic. The addition of a bit of lime at planting will be helpful if your soil is mildly acidic.

*Dicentra eximia* 'Luxuriant' blooms gaily in a shady garden.

*Dicentra* 'Luxuriant' is attractive with a dark-leaved ground cover of bugleweed (*Ajuga reptans* 'Back Scallop') in a deeply shaded garden.

## *Euphorbia griffithii* 'Fireglow'
### Griffith's Spurge

This brightly colored plant is dazzling from the moment its reddish-orange asparagus-like stems shoot out of the soil in spring until the snow covers its brilliant fall foliage. Leaves emerge green with a subtle hint of orange and red midveins turning to orange-tinged gold as summer cools. The four-inch-wide tuft of "flowers" (these are actually bracts rather than true flowers) are scarlet with a touch of yellow. They are quite impressive above the greenish foliage but can't compete once the first hard frost causes the foliage to glow bright orange. In any of its stages 'Fireglow' is electrifying, especially so when paired with yellows or blues.

Foliage in transition from early-summer green to late-summer golden-orange displays a kaleidoscope of colors.

*Euphorbia griffithii* 'Dixter' holds center stage in a beautiful combination (design by Teena Garay).

*Euphorbia griffithii* 'Fireglow' in its midsummer finery.

The same scene after a frost has revealed brilliant fall colors.

Full sun
Moist, humus-rich soil
Interesting all season
Height 24–36", Width 36"
Zone 3 (officially Zone 4)

*Euphorbia griffithii* 'Fireglow' will develop into a large shrub-like clump about three feet tall and wide so give it plenty of room. Though some gardeners from Outside describe it as aggressive, I've found it easy to keep in bounds in our climate.

'Dixter' is another lovely cultivar of the same species. Its flowers are more orange and the foliage is darker and copper tinted. Its overall impact is a bit more subtle than *Euphorbia griffithii* 'Fireglow,' but it's a bit harder to find.

### *Filipendula rubra* 'Venusta'
#### Queen of the Prairie

At nearly eight feet in height, queen of the prairie (*Filipendula rubra* 'Venusta') is a statuesque plant with large, showy, and frothy pink panicles appearing mid-summer to late in the season. Flowers will persist until after the first hard freeze or you can cut them for drying. The leaves are nicely textured, medium-size, and amply arranged along the stem from close to the ground to about one foot below the flowers. The absence of leaves near the top of the flower spikes adds more emphasis to the wonderfully full blooms and makes them easy to arrange in a vase. Better yet, this attention-getting plant stands tall even in windy locations without assistance of any kind.

*Filipendula rubra* 'Venusta' is a resilient, easy-to-grow plant that can be used as a sublime focal point or at the back of a large garden. It is equally at home as a member of a cottage garden or a more formal one. Lots of sun, a bit of humus in the soil, and consistent water are all you need to keep this stellar selection happy. My ten-year-old clump shows no sign of needing dividing. On the other hand, you can easily propagate *Filipendula rubra* 'Venusta' by taking plantlets from around the edges of the main clump. This selection can also be grown in boggy areas, where it will spread somewhat more rapidly.

Full sun to part shade

Moist, well-draining to somewhat-boggy humus-rich soil

Summer into fall

Height 8', Width 4'

Zone 3

A closely related species is *Filipendula ulmaria*, commonly known as queen of the meadow. It has a mass of white fluffy flowers at the terminus of each flower spike. Foliage, horticultural needs, resistance to wind, and uses are similar, though it is a bit shorter in stature and blooms a little earlier than *Filipendula rubra* 'Venusta.'

Clockwise:

Frothy pink plumes are reminiscent of cotton candy when in full bloom.

*Filipendula rubra* 'Venusta' stands tall with 'Diablo' ninebark (*Physocarpus opulifolius* 'Diablo') in the foreground.

*Filipendula ulmaria* provides a protective backdrop for one of the benches in the Serenity Garden at South Peninsula Hospital in Homer, Alaska.

### *Iris sibirica, Iris setosa, Iris pseudacorus,* and *Iris pumila*

Siberian Iris, Native Iris, Yellow Flag Iris, and Dwarf Iris

Iris is a real stalwart in a Far North garden. The hardy members of this group of plants are easy to grow and most are readily available. Its distinctive sword-like foliage attracts your eye, making iris an excellent plant to place periodically throughout the garden bed to establish cohesion through repetition. The strong vertical profile of iris foliage is a perfect contrast to either frilly, deeply cut foliage or big, bold leaves. Flamboyant, complex blossoms, available in a wide range of colors, including some bicolor varieties, light up the garden when they burst forth. Though the floral display of a given species is not as protracted as that of some long-blooming perennials, the relatively large size and unusual shape of each iris flower compels us to pay attention to it. If you make your selections with care, you can have iris blooming in early spring, midsummer, and late summer. Cutting back the flower stalk to near the ground when the bloom is spent will encourage revitalization of the rhizome (fleshy root) and occasionally leads to a second round of flowers.

✻✻✻

*Iris sibirica* 'Caesar's Brother' mingles with Himalayan blue poppies (*Meconopsis betonicifolia*).

*Iris sibirica* 'Silver Edge.'

*Iris sibirica* or Siberian iris is native to moist meadows, but for Far North gardeners it actually does better in an average garden environment than in very wet areas. Its height varies between two and four feet depending on the cultivar (cultivated variety). Colors include many shades of blue and purple as well as burgundy, pink, white, and yellow, sometimes in combination. There are

Full sun to part shade

Tolerant of a range of soils, but does best in moist, well-drained acidic soil

Blooms in midsummer

Height 24–48", Width 16–36"

Zone 3 (officially a few varieties are Zone 4)

literally hundreds of varieties and cultivars from which to choose. Each stem bears several blooms that open successively. 'Silver Edge' is a sturdy selection in rich purple-blue with a sliver of white along the edges of each petal. The blossoms are very large and striking. 'Caesar's Brother' is one of the tallest cultivars with exceptionally narrow, almost grass-like leaves and purple flowers held high above the foliage. 'Ruffled Velvet' is deep burgundy with delightful wavy falls (the parts of the flower that hang down). Most Siberian irises bloom during midsummer, with the taller varieties blooming a bit later.

❉ ❉ ❉

Alaska is home to a lovely midsize iris, *Iris setosa*. In some parts of the world it is commonly referred to as blue flag iris or wild iris; here it's often called native iris. The flower color varies somewhat from blue to purple and occasionally lavender. Masses of blooms typically open in June followed by large, knobby seed pods that are useful in dried arrangements. This local iris inhabits the shores of lakes

Full sun to part shade

Tolerant of a range of soils, best in humus-rich, moist, well-drained acidic soil

Blooms early summer

Height 6–24", Width 15–24"

Zone 2 (officially Zone 3)

and streams in the wild so will accommodate a similar environment in your garden. Interestingly, it also thrives in a fast-draining rock garden as can be seen in the image (right). That's a wide range of environments. *Iris setosa* forms full, lush clumps and is trouble-free and tolerant of salt air and wind, growing wild even in the Aleutian Islands.

A pretty white Siberian iris given to me by homesteader Ann Gillas.

A mass of *Iris setosa* in full bloom commands attention in this rock garden near a small stream.

❉ ❉ ❉

A single blossom of yellow flag iris (*Iris pseudacorus*) asserts itself in a lush planting. The bold vertical foliage adds a strong architectural statement.

A large clump of deep-burgundy *Iris pumila* 'Candy Apple' is spectacular in spring.

*Iris pseudacorus* or yellow flag iris is a tall, robust plant with substantial, sword-like foliage and bright, soft-yellow flowers; it definitely demands notice. This species performs well in a normal garden environment but excels in bogs, at the margin of a marsh, or standing in shallow water. A large clump of yellow flag iris in a pond is breathtaking. It blooms late in the season, usually unfurling from mid-August to early September. A variegated variety has even more striking foliage but is not quite as vigorous as the species.

Full sun to part shade

Acidic soil with average moisture content to standing water

Blooms late summer into September

Height 48", Width 24–30"

Zone 3 (officially Zone 5)

The shortest but showiest of the hardy irises is *Iris pumila*, or miniature dwarf bearded iris. These spring-blooming lovelies with their large, elaborate blossoms are available in a rainbow of solid colors like rich burgundy 'Candy Apple' and soft peach 'Betsy Boo' as well as dramatic combinations like 'Navy Doll,' which is creamy white with a splash of dark blue and touch of yellow, and the bright orange with gold of 'Mauhaus.' To increase the impact of these wonderful colors arrange *Iris pumila* in good-sized clumps. The gray-green leaves are barely six inches tall and nearly one inch wide, but still strongly vertical. Dwarf iris is stunning in combination with spring-blooming bulbs and always a welcome addition to the garden. Plant rhizomes so close to the surface they are barely covered in well-drained soil.

Full sun to part shade

Average to dry acidic soil

Blooms in June

Height 6–10", Width 16–24"

Zone 3 (officially Zone 4)

### *Nepeta racemosa* 'Walker's Low'
### 'Walker's Low' Catmint

Drought-tolerant, exuberant, and long-blooming 'Walker's Low' catmint is an excellent garden plant that's easy to grow and care for. Small, soft, fuzzy, gray-green, slightly aromatic foliage and lavender-blue flower spikes blend beautifully with a wide range of colors and styles. 'Walker's Low' catmint has a relaxed habit and form that makes it quite at home in informal gardens, but it also has applicability in more formal settings. It is delightful as an edging plant, especially along a walkway or path where passersby might release its gentle fragrance as they brush against it. When planted under long-legged shrubs and roses or in rock gardens, the billowy form of this plant adds a lovely softness to the scene. Named Plant of the Year in 2007 by the Perennial Plant Association, *Nepeta racemosa* 'Walker's Low' thrives in a wide range of environments, is pest and disease resistant, and is very low maintenance. Though from the same family as catnip, this selection should not attract the local felines. In Far North gardens, it is a great replacement for the much less hardy lavender.

Full sun

Lean, fast-draining soil to humus-rich, moist, well-draining soil

Blooms mid-June through September

Height 30", Width 36"

Zone 3

Billowy and drought-tolerant *Nepeta racemosa* 'Walker's Low' enlivens a south-sloping rock garden.

A large clump of 'Walker's Low' catmint mingles nicely with bold reds and tall grasses.

One of the candelabra primroses, *Primula waltonii* has a graceful, quiet charm.

### Primula

**Primrose, Cowslip**

Primroses absolutely thrive in our relatively cool and moist summer climate. The ease with which we can successfully grow this delightful genus is one of the great gifts of northern gardening. With more than four hundred options available, there will surely be a primrose that steals your heart and suits your site. If you find this group of plants to your liking, you can find additional information in books and societies dedicated to *Primula*.

Most *Primula* prefer humus-rich, moist, well-drained soil. At northern latitudes they can be grown in full sun or part shade. Because their foliage is of medium size, they provide a good contrast for either tiny leaves or big, bold ones. Their flowers have a delicate freshness that belies their hardy and robust nature. Many varieties also add a lovely fragrance to the garden. Their quiet charm makes them a natural in a woodland garden, along a path, or at the front of a border where they can be admired closely.

Many primroses have a rosette of low-growing, ovate, apple-green foliage. Spring-blooming pale-yellow *Primula juliae* 'Dorothy' holds her flowers just above the rosette, nearly obscuring the foliage with an incredible mass of blooms. *Primula juliae* 'Wanda' has pretty rosy-purple blossoms that are tucked in among the leaves. Both have a very noticeable dark-yellow eye at the center of each flower, offering you a second flower color to play with in your combinations.

In other primrose varieties, tall stems hold swirls of flowers high above the rosette of foliage. As a group these are referred to as candelabra primroses. Among these is the intensely fragrant, stately, two-foot-tall *Primula florindae* or Tibetan primrose. When the large planting of these near my pond comes into bloom its perfume fills the air, compelling garden visitors to seek the source of the heady scent. Tibetan primrose is usually available in sulfur yellow but can also

*Primula Resources*

American Primrose Society,
www.americanprimrosesociety.org

*Primula (Revised Edition)*,
by John Richards (Timber Press)

Full sun to part shade

Moist, well-drained, humus-rich soil

Blooming period depends on the species—see narrative for details

Height 2–30", Width 4–18", both depending on species

Zones 3–5. All primroses mentioned here are hardy to Zone 3.

be found in a delicate and hauntingly attractive rust color. It blooms for an extended time from midsummer into September.

*Primula auricula* has fleshier, more compact foliage. It is an early bloomer and does well in rock gardens and other fast-draining environments. Flowers can be solid bright yellow or deep purple around the edges with a yellow center. The two-toned ones are quite stunning when the colors are pure and intense. This species is very promiscuous in the garden, sometimes producing inferior offspring but occasionally creating a spectacular result. As a result it's best to purchase this species in bloom so you can see if you like the flower color of the plant before you buy it.

Clockwise:

*Primula denticulata* or drumstick primrose shows a bit of farinose, a whitish powder, near the top of its stems. Some primroses will have farinose on their flowers or the underside of their leaves. This is a naturally occurring phenomenon—not a problem.

The red buds of poker primrose (*Primula vialii*) open to lavender from the bottom of the flower, creating a two-toned effect.

*Primula denticulata* 'Ronsdorf Mix' in very early spring.

Long-blooming *Primula cortusoides* sports large clusters of warm-pink blossoms above pale-green foliage for much of the summer.

One of the most unusual primroses is poker primrose (*Primula vialii*), whose red buds open into lavender florets in late summer. The tiny flowers are arranged in a spear-shaped affair held above the traditional rosette of ovate foliage in late summer. The buds open from the bottom of the poker, creating a two-toned effect.

Drumstick primroses are among the earliest bloomers with their signature globe of flowers forming as the leaves first appear. Both the flower stalks and leaves continue to grow with time. 'Ronsdorf Mix' drumstick primrose can be as tall as one foot and offers a nice mix of white, purple, blue, rose, and medium-pink flowers.

### *Rheum palmatum* 'Atrosanguineum'
### Ornamental Rhubarb

Ornamental rhubarb dons so many costumes during the course of a season it's difficult to select a representative photograph. As the garden's first bulbs emerge in early spring, *Rheum palmatum* unfurls its massive, brilliant rose leaves to herald the new season. This rosy beginning foretells a bit about its finishing flourish, as the eight-foot-tall flower stalks that will appear in late summer are robed in the same hue. Between these two events, the foliage transitions to a rich, burgundy-infused green above with dark burgundy on the reverse. The slightest breeze will flutter the deeply cut two-to-three-foot leaves, creating a dazzling impact. This plant is a natural as a focal point; surrounded by bold neighbors it will still hold center stage. Few plants that enjoy full sun have such large foliage, making this one a designer's dream.

With deep burgundy on the reverse side of its leaves, *Rheum palamatum* 'Atrosanguineum' is a real standout among the ornamental rhubarbs.

Brilliant rose foliage emerges very early in the season.

Full sun to part shade

Moist, humus-rich soil

Interesting all season

Foliage height to 42", over-all height 8', Width 6'

Zone 3 (officially Zone 5)

Top, left to right:

With time and warmer temperatures the foliage changes color to burgundy-infused green on the upper side while the reverse turns deep burgundy.

The reverse of the leaves remain burgundy or purple throughout the season.

Bottom, left to right:

*Rheum palmatum*, the species, has the same size and leaf shape as *Rheum palmatum* 'Atrosanguineum' but not the intensity of color. Even so, it is still a wonderful architectural addition to any northern garden.

Stout, eight-foot tall, rose-clad flower spikes bring forth the grand finale.

At maturity *Rheum palmatum* 'Atrosanguineum,' the best of the cultivars, can exceed six feet in width so give it plenty of room. It's an excellent alternative to a medium-size shrub as it provides similar weight without the need for moose protection.

If you don't have enough space for this plant but desire a similar effect, consider using culinary rhubarb in your gardens. Though not as colorful or deeply cut, the foliage of edible rhubarb is also bold and substantial. It too enjoys full sun and will produce a tall flower spike usually in off-white. It comes with the added benefit that you can eat the delectable stems!

### *Viola* 'Etain'
#### Violet Hybrid

From early spring until after the first snow, *Viola* 'Etain' steadfastly produces cheery flowers with a delicate spicy fragrance. This remarkable longevity of bloom is matched by a wonderful versatility, though this plant can be somewhat short-lived. *Viola* 'Etain' is at home in rock gardens, a perfect choice for containers, and even more robust at the front of a well-tended, humus-rich border. I often use them in containers for a season then plant them into the garden. Try them along a walkway or near your deck so you can enjoy their joyful faces. Though optional in terms of plant health, deadheading will increase the amount and vibrancy of flowers throughout the season.

Full sun to part shade

Prefers fertile, humus-rich, well-drained soil

Blooms June through September

Height 6", Width 10"

Zone 3 (officially Zone 4)

*Viola* 'Etain' is a perennial favorite and quickly sells out at local nurseries. There is a bit of variation in the amount of lavender in any given plant. Offspring may be more yellow or exhibit more purple than the parent plant. All are delightful additions to any garden.

In full bloom just after the crocus have finished and the daffodils begin to open, *Viola* 'Etain' will still be going strong when the snow flies.

Charming, long-lasting, soft-yellow faces trimmed in lavender have a spicy fragrance.

Foxtail grass delivers a brilliant hot combination with 'Paprika' yarrow (*Achillea millefolium* 'Paprika').

### *Alopecurus pratensis* 'Aureovariegatus'
Foxtail Grass

Foxtail grass is the perfect hardy alternative for one of the most popular shade-tolerant grasses used outside Alaska. That popular grass, Japanese forest grass (*Hakonechloa macra* 'Aureola'), is not hardy enough for the Far North, but its golden tresses and spilling form are very desirable. No need to be disappointed, though, as we have an even better option—the wonderful *Alopecurus pratensis* 'Aureovariegatus.' It is incredibly hardy and is equally happy in part shade and sun. In shade it spills over in a fountain-like silhouette; in sun it is more upright and spiky. In both cases its gleaming, variegated green-and-gold foliage draws attention.

By late summer its colors are more muted and golden, even picking up a few burgundy highlights.

In early spring *Alopecurus pratensis* 'Aureovariegatus' is distinctly green and yellow.

*Alopecurus pratensis 'Aureovariegatus' takes on a softer, more fountain-like profile in part shade.*

This versatile grass can be used as an edging or to frame a path or entrance. It complements and coordinates well with a vast range of colors, showing off the blooms of nearby flowering plants. It glows when backlit and is eye-catching enough to be effective as a repetitive theme in a large garden. It is clump forming and is a cool-season grass, ideally suited to Alaska's climate.

Full sun to part shade

Grow in fertile, well-drained soil

Interesting all season long. Inflorescences appear midseason; some prefer to cut them to keep the focus on the foliage.

Height 2–3', Width 16"

Zone 3 (officially Zone 5)

### *Deschampsia cespitosa* 'Bronzeschleier'
**Bronze Veil Tufted Hair Grass**

Though it's neither the showiest nor the most colorful of the hardy grasses, if I were limited to only one kind of grass forever more in my gardens, I'd choose *Deschampsia cespitosa* 'Bronzeschleier' to be the one. The threadlike, medium-green foliage of this special grass has incredibly fine texture. It has a gracefully arching form and wispy bronze inflorescences that reach out beyond the mound of foliage. The flowers are a nice addition to mixed cut arrangements and have a long vase life. A mature clump of bronze veil hair grass will exceed four feet in width, giving it enough presence to be used as a focal point. On the other hand, its understated beauty makes this grass an amiable companion in myriad situations.

Full sun to part shade

Tolerates soil from dry to moist, acidic to neutral

Attractive all season

Height 4', Width 4'

Zone 3 (officially Zone 5)

Its tolerant disposition extends to the range of conditions in which *Deschampsia cespitosa* can be grown successfully. It will do fine in the relatively dry environment of a rock garden, though will appreciate some humus being added to the soil in that case. It thrives in moist, well-drained, or continually damp soils, whether they are neutral or acidic. And finally, it is happy in sun or part shade. That covers a lot of territory!

This is a cool-season grass that has proven itself hardy to zone 3, though the literature often lists it (as well as many other grasses) as zone 5. Cut it back in early spring. It can be propagated easily by division.

Bronze veil hair grass (*Deschampsia cespitosa* 'Bronzeschleier') forms a graceful mound with gently swaying bronze flowers floating above. *Clematis tangutica* climbs a trellis in the background.

Lovely soft bronze inflorescences subtly replay the dark foliage of 'Victor Reiter' geranium (*Geranium pratense* 'Victor Reiter') and deep-rose blossoms of petunia 'Pretty Much Picasso.'

The soft gray-green and pale-ivory leaves and ruddy stems of *Cornus alba* 'Bailhalo' bring out an inviting contrast and subtle echo with the deep-purple foliage of *Actaea simplex* 'Hillside Black Beauty' in the author's garden.

### *Cornus alba* 'Bailhalo' and *Cornus alba* 'Elegantissima'
#### Variegated Redtwig Dogwood

Redtwig dogwoods are vigorous, dependable, and delightful four-season deciduous shrubs. When taller than your winter snow level, their dark red stems sparkle vividly on a sunny winter day. In spring flat clusters of white flowers are dainty but enjoyable. 'Bailhalo' and 'Elegantissima' dogwoods have lovely gray-green foliage with irregular ivory margins, making them exceedingly versatile members of a mixed perennial garden. There is little difference between the two except size. 'Bailhalo' is a dwarf at three feet in height and width while 'Elegantissima' will grow to ten feet in both directions.

It will take some time for either to reach its maximum size, so purchase the largest specimen you can at the outset. Younger stems are redder than older ones. To increase the dazzling effect of your twigs, cut back a third of the oldest wood to just above the crown in early spring each year. Moose will definitely sample this shrub so do protect it in winter.

Variegated redtwig dogwood foliage adds a luminous accent to a dark corner of a shady garden.

Full sun to part shade, though stems have better color in full sun

Prefers humus-rich, well-drained, slightly acidic soil

Attractive year-round

Height 3' or 10', Width 3' or 10'

Zone 2

### *Physocarpus opulifolius* 'Dart's Gold'
Golden Ninebark

*Physocarpus opulifolious* or ninebark is most commonly known for its popular purple-leaved cultivar 'Diablo.' While 'Dart's Gold' shares the pleasing three-lobed leaf shape of its close relative, it is much more assertive in both color and vigor. 'Dart's Gold' will leaf out considerably earlier than its darker cousins

The brilliant chartreuse foliage of 'Dart's Gold' ninebark stands out among a chorus of notable leafy neighbors.

Full sun to part shade

Fertile, moist, well-draining acidic soil

Blooms in spring, interesting all season

Height 6', Width to 8'

Zone 3

and attain mature size sooner. Given the shortness of our season, this earlier awakening is a distinct advantage.

Like many shrubs this one can be used both at the back of the border as well as mixed among large perennials. Its somewhat cascading form also gives you the opportunity to employ it near the front of the garden bed as shown in the photo at left. Its bright golden hue makes 'Dart's Gold' prominent in shady gardens and a gleaming centerpiece in sun. It combines well with dark and well-saturated colors and more subtly with variegated green-and-gold companions.

If you desire a dark-leafed shrub, try 'Center Glow' ninebark (*Physocarpus opulifolius* 'Center Glow'). Its deep color is infused with just a hint of orange, making the deep shade of its mature foliage quite lively while the newer leaves do in fact glow.

Both varieties have peeling bark and dense corymbs of white spring flowers, and spread slowly by suckers. Protect them from winter-browsing moose.

Close-up view of *Physocarpus opulifolious* 'Center Glow' displays the luminous newer foliage from which this variety draws its name. (Photo courtesy of Christine Wickham)

*Clematis recta* 'Purpurea' has a
sweet fragrance and attractive
foliage (design by Teena Garay).

### *Clematis recta* 'Purpurea Select' and *Clematis tangutica*
Clematis, Russian Virgin's Bower, Old Man's Beard

Sometimes called the queen of the vines, clematis is available in a vast range of sizes and bloom types. Each has its own unique charm, though the pruning regimens can be confusing and somewhat unsettling. Because we share our gardens with moose, there's an advantage in selecting varieties that bloom on the current year's growth. The two recommended here are among those that do so.

*Clematis recta* 'Pupurea' is a diminutive and dainty option with single, star-shaped, fragrant white flowers dancing along the ends of branches covered in pretty bronze-tinted foliage. At barely six feet in height, this selection is perfect for smaller gardens. It needs support to stay upright.

*Clematis tangutica* is big, bold, long blooming, and brash. Its bright yellow bell-shaped blossoms resemble little lanterns appearing in abundance from midsummer until fall. As each flower fades it is replaced by an equally delightful fluffy seed head. These seed heads engender the perfectly appropriate nickname old man's beard. *Clematis tangutica* is vigorous and large. It will grow to twenty feet in height and six to ten feet in width, so give it plenty of room and a stout support upon which to climb. I have found this variety to be one of the most dependably hardy, though it is listed as Zone 6 in many texts.

Bright-yellow lantern-like blossoms mingle with fluffy silvery seed heads on *Clematis tangutica*.

Full sun

Humus-rich, well-drained soil

Summer to fall

Height 6', Width 3' (*Clematis recta* 'Purpurea Select'), Height 20', Width to 10' (*Clematis tangutica*)

Zone 3 (officially Zone 6 for *C. tangutica*)

You will often see an admonishment to shade the roots of clematis so they don't get too hot. Cold soils and a cool climate make this guidance of little concern for Alaska gardeners.

My mother's favorite, the
beautiful Peace Rose.

Like nearly every gardener I know, my love of gardening was inspired by someone else. In my case it was my mother. She was a wonderful gardener who could seemingly grow anything and did. Mother gardened in Philadelphia, a city with a mild climate that one might think would make gardening easy. Well, it *is* easier than in Alaska, but within her sphere, Mother was the best. All of her friends and acquaintances sought her advice on how to "slip" a rose, how to grow tomatoes that tasted exactly like hers, and how to replicate the stunning results she achieved in her gardens. She grew big, flavorful vegetables and beautiful, lush perennials. Her rose garden was truly something special to behold. Her favorite rose was the heavenly scented Peace Rose (*Rosa* 'Madame A. Meilland') with its lovely, soft yellow petals edged in warm peachy-apricot.

From my earliest memory my mother constantly encouraged me to learn about plants as well as to appreciate their beauty. When I was two she gave me a pail and my very own trowel so I could "garden" by her side as she worked among her plants and talked to me about what she was doing. I'm quite sure my efforts as a two-year-old weren't terribly helpful, but she never let on.

All during my childhood, Mother and I went for long morning walks together in Fairmount Park, a huge, largely wooded public park within the city limits of Philadelphia. To this day it has extensive gardens and walkways lined with graceful flowering trees as well as beautifully landscaped parkways enjoyed by commuters, exercise enthusiasts, and people out for an afternoon or evening stroll. It also has vast wild areas of natural native vegetation where Mother showed me the locations of "her" secret wild berry bushes. She taught me the common names of the plants as we explored along the paths. She might not have known their botanical names, but she sure knew everything else about the plants in her realm.

It was in the wild parts of Fairmount Park where, when I was old enough to go alone, I picked special bouquets of flowers for my mother. I knew the location of a big patch of lovely woodland violets and would carefully gather some for her each spring. Then I'd run home as fast as my short young legs would carry me with the delicate flowers clutched gently in my grubby little fingers. Mother would smile with pure delight when I offered up my gift. Her pleasure exhilarated me. It also laid the foundation for my understanding of how important and magical flowers can be in our lives.

My mother grew the best-tasting tomatoes I have ever eaten, bar none. I can still conjure up the smell and taste of a warm heirloom tomato pulled from one of her vines and eaten right on the spot in the garden. I can feel the bright red juice

This is part of the thriving natural meadow on our land near Homer, Alaska.

that ran between my fingers as I sank my teeth into its firm flesh. I keep trying to replicate that flavor in my own greenhouse in Alaska, but I fear it's not to be, even though I've grown the same varieties she did. I've even planted a fish head or two beneath each vine as was her practice for all of her tomatoes. Well, maybe salmon don't do the same job as bluefish from the Atlantic. Or perhaps my memory exaggerates the flavor of her tomatoes. Whatever it is, my tomatoes don't compare to my memory of hers, but I still think of her every time I pick a ripe, juicy tomato from one of my vines. I do wish now that I had paid more attention to all of her tomato-growing rituals and secrets.

In fact, I wish I had paid more attention to *everything* Mother did in her garden! As much as I enjoyed being with her as a preteen, I was headed for a career in business and, sadly, as a teenager I became quite disdainful of anything domestic. Fortunately, I had already developed a love of plants, the knowledge of how they can bring joy to people, and how much fun it is to thrust your hands into rich, fertile soil and try to create something enchanting and beautiful.

While I concentrated on my business career, these seeds of knowledge lay dormant as if under a blanket of snow waiting for an elusive spring. During those years, I always had gardens, but I didn't have much time to devote to any of them. I usually designed them, but hired other folks to install and maintain them for me. I did, of course, enjoy their beauty and the atmosphere they created, but I missed the sheer joy of nurturing my plants, observing their progress, and seeing the myriad nuanced changes that seem to occur daily in a richly planted garden.

When my husband and I retired from the computer industry in 1991 and moved to Alaska, we built a house outside of Homer, on a south-facing and sloping piece of land with a breathtaking view of Kachemak Bay. The property was blessed with a wonderful meadow of wildflowers surrounded by vast stands of towering old spruce trees. We asked the builders to minimize the area in which they disturbed the native vegetation. I wanted a totally natural space as I had no intention of starting a garden.

I planned to spend my time learning about and exploring all that Alaska offered. I had big-picture things in mind—a trip up the Dalton Highway to Prudhoe Bay, a cruise on Glacier Bay, fishing in the Gulf of Alaska and Kachemak Bay, and hiking in the hills around Homer. Then I met Elizabeth Shaw.

Elizabeth lived nearby and had a delightful garden, designed so her young family and black lab, Jet, had plenty of room to romp. The entrance to their home wound up through a series of garden beds constructed with rustic railroad ties used to tame the steep grade of their lot. Each section had a novel and vibrant color scheme that commanded your attention as you passed by. If you dallied, you might also spot clever little mementos tucked among her plants. A tumble of incredibly colorful annuals spilled from an array of containers on her deck each summer. Every time my husband and I went to visit Elizabeth and her husband, Alan, I found myself gushing about the abundance and appeal of her flowers. Elizabeth invariably encouraged me to start an Alaska garden myself, but I went fishing instead!

Battered and worn, the original container from Elizabeth Shaw still does duty on our deck.

Then one day, Alan showed up in our driveway with a wooden planter box crammed with jubilant annuals in full bloom. "Elizabeth said you need this," was all he said as he put the box filled with beauty on our deck. Well, that did it! Elizabeth's gift immediately changed the entire mood of our deck and, though I didn't realize it at the time, eventually changed my life. I loved the way the bright annuals added a vibrant splash of color, blooming diligently throughout the summer. All those childhood memories of the joy of flowers came rushing back to fill my head and stimulate my imagination. It didn't take much time for me to realize that I wanted more of these vivid, exuberant, and captivating plants in my Alaska life.

Our local building supply store sells old whiskey barrels that have been cut in half. They are ubiquitous in Alaska. They can be seen in front of businesses, on sidewalks, near the front door of residences from Fairbanks to Juneau, and scattered about gardens throughout the state. One of these seemed a practical container for more flowers. Soon, four seemed an even better idea than just one. There are now nine flower-filled half barrels on our front deck. Another collection frames our entry porch. And if

Whiskey barrels are often employed as easy-care containers for summer color.

you count the ones scattered in my perennial gardens, there are twenty-two barrels altogether, all crammed full of plants spring, summer, and fall. Whiskey barrels have turned out be a very fortuitous choice as they are spacious enough to accept a wide range of plants and substantial enough that the watering schedule is not burdensome. They also complement the rustic style of much of Alaska's architecture and that of our cedar-sided home. Don't get me wrong—I admire the look of a group of interesting clay or ceramic pots, and have tons of these now too, but I was not yet an Alaska Gardener with a capital *G*. I was decorating my deck with pretty flowers, but I still wanted this endeavor to be so easy that it would take very little of my time, since other Alaska adventures continued to beckon.

Then one spring, while searching for more varied plants to add to my annual displays, I visited Fritz Creek Gardens, at the time a new nursery in our area. When I asked about annuals, Rita Jo Shoultz, who owned the nursery, explained that she was selling perennials, not annuals. I don't know how my future revealed itself so clearly to her. However, I can still see the wry smile that flickered across her face when I declared that annuals were *it* for me. "Please come back when you change your mind about that," she said prophetically. I did and we are now close friends.

She had said "when," not "if," and was she ever right! One thing has led to another. I now have, at this writing, nine different garden beds filled with hundreds of different kinds of perennial plants. I also have an herb garden, a greenhouse, a water garden, and two large raised vegetable patches. Of course, Elizabeth's original planter and all the whiskey barrels full of annuals are still in place, too. It was, after all, Elizabeth's generous act of friendship that heralded the inception of an obsession that continues to grow.

Her gift also began to illustrate for me that to fully understand life in the Far North, I needed a garden. Gardening made the restorative benefits of the seasons, not just their beauty, vitally clear. The amazing accomplishments of Alaska pioneers who carved homes and livelihoods out of a wild land in an unforgiving climate were

A half whiskey barrel overflowing with lemon-yellow African daisies (*Osteospermum*) brightens the deck.

A darling spring calf looks my way before scampering to her mother.

revealed with clarity and in unexpected ways once I turned my hand to an Alaska garden. It has been enormously enriching.

Gardens are now my passion. I cherish the time I can spend in them. Learning more about new plants, soil chemistry, and using beneficial insects to control pests so I can create healthier gardens stimulates my mind. My winters are spent devouring gardening books and designing new gardens. In my quest for better understanding I took a Master Gardeners course, did my volunteer hours, and became a Master Gardener. I joined the Homer Garden Club and eventually served as its president for six years. The garden club and other gardening activities have given me the opportunity to meet kindred spirits, many of whom have become close and dear friends. Our shared experiences—frustration over a late spring or a moose-eaten tree, pleasure from a bountiful harvest, excitement about a well-chosen combination of plants, pride in showing off our gardens to fellow gardeners who truly understand what it took to achieve—infuse our friendships with the ardor of youth and add another layer of appreciation to our bonds.

Gardens By Design, the design, installation, and maintenance company I founded, has also introduced me to wonderful people, many of whom have become great friends. They've given me the opportunity to design and create well over one hundred and fifty gardens and each has taught me something new. Through this work I've been able to produce and maintain gardens in environments far different from my own. These range from small kitchen gardens to very large commercial installations. I've experimented with plants some said wouldn't grow here and found that they will, at least in the right microclimate. Designing new gardens, creating innovative combinations, learning much more about gardening in Alaska, and even learning botanical names have brought me incredible pleasure and fulfillment. Much of what I know has come from the generous, giving spirit of other gardeners and I thank them all for what they have shared and counseled. In the Alaska tradition of sharing what one has, I offer the fruits of my experiences to you in this book. I hope you enjoy it.

# Works Consulted


Armitage, Allan M. 2008. *Herbaceous Perennial Plants.* Athens: University of Georgia Press.

Brickell, Christopher, and Judith D. Zuk, eds. 1997. *The American Horticultural Society A–Z Encyclopedia of Garden Plants.* New York: DK Publishing, Inc.

Burrell, C. Colston. 1999. *Perennial Combinations: Stunning Combinations That Make Your Garden Look Fantastic Right from the Start.* Emmaus, PA: Rodale Press, Inc.

Cooperative Extension Service University of Alaska. 2010. *Sustainable Gardening.* Fairbanks: University of Alaska Press.

DiSabato-Aust, Tracy. 2003. *The Well-Designed Mixed Garden.* Portland, OR: Timber Press.

Fell, Derek. 2007. *Encyclopedia of Hardy Plants.* Buffalo, NY: Firefly Books.

Hedla, Lenore. 1994. *The Alaska Gardener's Handbook.* Anchorage, AK: High North Press.

Homer Garden Club. 2005. *Kachemak Cultivating from Seaside to Summit.* Audubon, IA: Audubon Media Corporation.

McGary, Jane, ed. 2003. *Rock Garden Design and Construction.* Portland, OR: Timber Press.

National Resources Conservation Service. "Chapter 1: The Soil Food Web." In *Soil Biology Primer.* www.soils.usda.gov/sqi/concepts/soil_biology/soil_food_web.html.

Phillips, Ellen, and C. Colston Burrell. 1993. *Rodale's Illustrated Encyclopedia of Perennials.* Emmaus, PA: Rodale Press.

Pratt, Verna E. 1991. *Wildflowers Along the Alaska Highway.* Anchorage, AK: Alaskakrafts.

Smith, P. Allen. 2006. *Colors for the Garden.* New York: Clarkson Potter/Publishers.

United States Department of Agriculture Agricultural Resource Service. USDA Plant Hardiness Zone Map. http://planthardiness.ars.usda.gov/PHZMWeb/.

University of Alaska Fairbanks Cooperative Extension Service. Publications catalog. www.uaf.edu/ces/pubs/catalog/.

Page numbers in *italics* indicate photos.

Thank you, Elizabeth, for your gift that changed my life.